THE
STRING TEACHER'S
COOKBOOK

Creative Recipes
for a Successful Program

Published by
Meredith Music Publications
a division of G.W. Music, Inc.
4899 Lerch Creek Ct., Galesville, MD 20765
http://www.meredithmusic.com

MEREDITH MUSIC PUBLICATIONS and its stylized double M logo are trademarks of
MEREDITH MUSIC PUBLICATIONS, a division of G.W. Music, Inc.

International Standard Book Number: 978-1-57463-091-6
Library of Congress Control Number: 2007938336
Printed and bound in U.S.A.

Contents

Foreword

When Gar Whaley, President of Meredith Music Publications, called to ask if I would compile a "cookbook" using recipes to describe tried-and-true techniques for string teaching, I jumped at the chance. I realized immediately that I would have the opportunity to learn from many experts in the field, and it would be a creative and fun project. What I didn't anticipate was that I would be receiving one of the most powerful and enlightening learning experiences of my career.

You may be thinking, "What's this, *another* cookbook? How did it get mixed in with the music books?" or "Not another book about how to teach!" To extend the cookbook analogy, however, the best recipes in my family are not the only good ones ever created. We have wonderfully delicious family recipes that have been passed down for generations. But I've also experimented with recipes from well-known chefs and local cooks for many years, seeking new ideas and flavors for variety in my life's experience. With each new recipe that I've tried, I've been able to decide whether to add the recipe to my folder of favorites, replace a traditional family recipe in favor of a new one, or reject the new recipe for one that I think is better, all with the help of my family's opinions on what worked or didn't work for them.

This is the essence of *The String Teacher's Cookbook: Creative Recipes for a Successful Program*. Fifty-seven experts in string teaching have written down their best ideas. Their only instruction was to choose a topic they are *passionate* about. By reading this book you will be able to try these experts' recipes and decide which ones work best for you and your students. Their personalities show in their writing styles, and their enthusiasm for affecting the lives of their students is evident. The authors come from many backgrounds of expertise. They are Suzuki teachers, public school elementary, middle, and high school teachers, private studio teachers, college professors, and world-class performers. All royalties from this book will benefit the American String Teachers Association (ASTA), a non-profit association dedicated to advancing string education. ASTA serves more than 11,500 members from throughout the string profession, providing a vast array of services and support to string educators and performers. Thanks to national ASTA presidents Robert Gillespie and Mary Wagner for making this possible. All authors have freely contributed their time, expertise, and energies to benefit students, teachers, parents, administrators, and audiences. Thanks to everyone for the wonderful contributions!

I challenge you to add some spice to your life by experimenting with these recipes.

Bon Appétit!

Joanne May
Project Director/Editor

Acknowledgments

To each of the *chefs* who contributed to this publication, I offer my sincere thanks. Each individual responded to our initial invitation with a resounding yes. They were each enthusiastic about being involved in what they felt would be a unique and worthwhile contribution to string playing and to music education. Their generosity has been exceptional, their expertise unquestionable and their love of string playing and music education inspiring. The writings within, presented by them, are based on years of study and experience from a variety of educational and professional levels.

Profound thanks and admiration are extended to Joanne May, editor and coordinator of this volume. Joanne could, and should, write a book on organization and management; her skills are incredible! She is a creative and talented individual to whom I owe a great deal of thanks for her tireless work on this project. Joanne went about the task of selecting authors, organizing and collecting materials, motivating writers and editing text with energy and enthusiasm. In addition to being a superb musician, Joanne is also an educator of the highest order which is apparent in the composition of this volume. Thanks to Joanne May, the world now has a collection of interesting and insightful articles contained in one volume written by many of today's most outstanding string players and pedagogues. To Shawn Girsberger my unending gratitude for her work with Meredith Music Publications and for the artistic layout and cover design of this volume. For leading the way in support of music education in our schools and for their assistance in marketing, thanks to the American String Teachers Association (ASTA), a non-profit association dedicated to advancing string education. ASTA serves more than 11,500 members from throughout the string profession, providing a vast array of services and support to string educators and performers. To learn more, go to www.astaweb.com

And finally, to the thousands of music students and their directors who have inspired each of us, our never-ending thanks for your dedication, beautiful music making and the belief that music does make a difference.

Garwood Whaley
President and Founder,
Meredith Music Publications

ക ക ക

About the Authors

Gilda Barston is Dean Emeritus of the Music Institute of Chicago, where she teaches cello to a class of students ranging in age from 4 years to adult. A graduate of the Juilliard School of Music, where she studied cello with Leonard Rose, Ms. Barston is a Registered Teacher Trainer in the Suzuki Method. Ms. Barston was on the faculty of the DePaul University School of Music for over twenty-five years, and currently teaches Suzuki pedagogy at Northwestern University. She is a past chair of the Suzuki Association of the Americas and the International Suzuki Association, and she is currently active on the ISA Board of Directors.

Susan E. Basalik has been a stringed instrument teacher in the Methacton School District in Norristown, Penn. since 1981. Her specialties are teaching elementary strings and using computer-assisted technology to enhance traditional teaching practices. Susan has presented technology sessions at local, state, and national conferences, including the American String Teachers Association Conference in 2006. She is a member of the Technology Institute for Music Educators (TI:ME), MENC, and ASTA, and is the current past-president of the Pennsylvania/Delaware chapter of ASTA.

Louis Bergonzi was appointed to the University of Illinois faculty in 2005. Prior to that appointment, he was on the faculty of the Eastman School of Music for sixteen years. Active as a clinician, adjudicator, and guest conductor of youth orchestras throughout the United States, Canada, Asia, and Australia, he has written for the *American String Teacher*, the *NSOA Newsletter*, and the *Journal of Research in Music Education*. He is coauthor of *Effects of Arts Education on Participation in the Arts* (National Endowment for the Arts, 1996) and of *Teaching Music Through Performance in Orchestra, Volumes 1 and 2* (GIA, 2002/2003). His *Rounds and Canons for Strings: Shaping Musical Independence* is published by Kjos Publishers. He is past-president of the American String Teachers Association (1998–2000).

Jeffrey S. Bishop is the director of orchestras at Shawnee Mission Northwest High School in suburban Kansas City. A published composer and author, Bishop has appeared nationally as a clinician at state, national, and international band and orchestra events. More information can be found at www.jeffreysbishop.com.

Muriel Bodley is a Suzuki teacher and public school teacher at Fayetteville-Manlius Schools in New York, teaching elementary and middle school orchestra. She is conductor of the Syracuse Symphony Youth String Orchestra, she was National School Orchestra Association Teacher of the Year in 1995, and she is a past-president of New York ASTA.

Judy Weigert Bossuat is the String Project Master Teacher at the California State University, Sacramento and serves on the National String Project Consortium. She is fomrerly instructor of string pedagogy at the University of Oregon in Eugene. Past-president of the California Chapter of ASTA, she was elected to the National ASTA Board in 2006. She is a graduate of SUNY Potsdam and the Talent Education Institute in Matsumoto, Japan where she studied with Shinichi Suzuki.

Mimi Butler (www.privatemusicstudio.com) teaches violin and viola privately to twenty-five to thirty students weekly in her Haddonfield, New Jersey home. Mimi is the author/publisher of *The Complete Guide to Running a Private Music Studio*, *The Complete Guide to Making More Money in the Private Music Studio* and her latest, *The Complete Guide to Raising Parents in the Private Music Studio*. Butler has been conducting workshops on the books throughout the country and in Canada and is a contributing writer for *Strad* magazine. The American String Teacher's Association, Southwest Strings, Lyon & Healy, and Woodwind & Brasswind also distribute the books.

Tanya Lesinsky Carey is professor emeritus of Western Illinois University and currently artist teacher at Roosevelt and DePaul Universities in Chicago and teaching pedagogy at the Cleveland Institute. The excellence of her students and her commitment to training teachers is well known in the profession. She is the author of the *Cello Playing is Easy* series on developing artistry, which is available through SHAR products.

Christina Castelli, international violin soloist, has performed with many of the world's leading orchestras, including those of Cleveland, Atlanta, Seattle, Pittsburgh, and Colorado, as well as Belgium, Colombia, and Chile. The only American native to be named a laureate of the 2001 Queen Elisabeth International Violin Competition, Ms. Castelli began studying the violin by the Suzuki method at age 3, later attending the Juilliard School, where she earned her master's degree and the program's highest honor, the William Schuman Prize. Ms. Castelli currently resides in New York City and enjoys a busy schedule of performing, teaching a select group of students, and presenting master classes for musicians.

Lisa Cridge teaches in Arlington, Virginia, is Principal Second in the National Gallery Chamber Orchestra, and also performs with the National Phil. She earned a B.M. from the Hartt School and a M.M. from the U. Memphis and played with the Memphis Symphony. Lisa has taught workshops at Catholic U., Dartmouth College, U. of Wisconsin at Appleton, and at the Blue Ridge Suzuki Camp. She is the author of *BOW GAMES and GOALS, I*, a spiral workbook of one hundred games for beginning violinists and violists. She can be reached at Soundpostpublish@aol.com

Winifred Crock is the orchestra director at Parkway Central High in Chesterfield, Missouri., a Grammy Gold Signature School. Mrs. Crock maintains a private violin studio in suburban St. Louis, Missouri and has been named Missouri ASTA Private Studio Teacher of the Year. She is a frequent guest clinician, conductor, and lecturer, and writes for the *Suzuki Journal of the Americas*.

Andrew H. Dabczynski, professor of music education at Brigham Young University, is an internationally recognized string music education specialist. He has vast experience as a public school and collegiate string/orchestra instructor, public school administrator, community music education coordinator, and performing violist/violinist. Dr. Dabczynski has appeared frequently as guest clinician, consultant, and conductor throughout the United States, Canada, Australia, New Zealand, and Mexico. He is coauthor of the *String Explorer* string method series, the *Fiddler's Philharmonic* series, and numerous arrangements for school orchestra.

Sandra Dackow is music director of the Hershey Symphony and president of the Conductors Guild. She holds bachelor and master of music degrees, as well as the doctor of philosophy degree from the Eastman School of Music. An Aspen Conducting fellow in 2001, she was also awarded the Silver Medal in the 2001 Vakhtang Jordania/New Millennium International Conducting Competition in Kharkov, Ukraine. An annual ASCAP award winning arranger, Dr. Dackow has generated over seventy works for young orchestras and is active as a guest conductor, adjudicator, and clinician across the US, as well as Canada, England, Hong Kong, South Africa, and throughout Australia and Ireland.

Jean Dexter (B.M., Michigan State, M.M.E., Southern Illinois-Edwardsville, specializing in the Suzuki Approach with John Kendall) is a Registered Teacher trainer with the Suzuki

Association of the Americas. Jean has twice served on the SAA board of directors, most recently as secretary, has served on SAA committees to develop systematic teacher training courses, and received the first Missouri ASTA Studio Teacher Award. Jean maintains a private Suzuki studio of cello and violin students in Olathe, Kansas.

Joanne Donnellan retired five years ago from teaching public school strings for thirty-three years in Ferndale, Washington. The last twenty-four years of her career were spent teaching 5th and 6th grade string classes in Ferndale's elementary schools, as well as leading its high school orchestra, where she had 129 students divided into four orchestra classes. Joanne has been the recipient of awards from WMEA and ASTA, including the ASTA Elizabeth A.H. Green School Educator Award in 2001, and most of all, she has a passion for teaching that will never go away! She still teaches privately and currently has thirteen violin students of various ages.

Patricia D'Ercole, a SAA-sanctioned Suzuki teacher trainer, teaches violin to children, and Suzuki pedagogy courses to graduate and undergraduate students at the Aber Suzuki Center at the University of Wisconsin-Stevens Point. She is an active clinician, teaching at many institutes in the US, Canada, Finland, Peru, and Chile. Pat has authored many articles for the *American Suzuki Journal*. She served on the Board of Directors for the Suzuki Association of the Americas and was the Board chair from 1997–1999.

Ian Edlund, after a distinguished thirty-eight-year teaching career, remains active as a cellist, clinician, and adjudicator. He also composes and arranges music for school orchestras, and directs the Birch Bay String Teachers' Workshop in Ferndale, Wash. He is recipient of the Elizabeth A. H. Green Award from the American String Teachers Association.

Teri Einfeldt is chair of the string and Suzuki departments of the University of Hartford's Hartt School of Music Community Division, and is on the violin faculty at the University of Hartford. Chair-Elect of the Suzuki Association of the Americas and an SAA registered Teacher Trainer, Teri is a frequent clinician at weekend string workshops and summer Suzuki institutes throughout the US, Puerto Rico, and Canada. In the past three years, Teri has been active in the use of video conferencing to promote teacher training to areas where training is not offered as a long-term option. Teri has recently completed a three-year term as a member of the board of directors of the Suzuki Association of the Americas.

Gerald Fischbach is professor of violin and string pedagogy at the University of Maryland, where he is director of graduate studies in music. A globe-trotting violinist, clinician, and conductor, Dr. Fischbach is also well known for his instructional videos, method books including *Artistry in Strings* and *Viva Vibrato!*, string arrangements, and articles on string pedagogy published in journals around the world. For thirty-three years, Dr. Fischbach ran the renowned summer seminar, International Workshops. He is a former president of the American String Teachers Association.

Kathy L. Fishburn has taught orchestra in Texas for more than thirty-seven years and is currently the orchestra director at Tascosa High School in Amarillo, Texas. Kathy is the executive director of the Greater Southwest Music Festival, and a past-president of the Texas Orchestra Directors Association, the Texas Music Educators Association, and the Texas Music Adjudicators Association. She also is the immediate past-president of the Texas Unit of the American String Teachers Association. Ms. Fishburn has many published arrangements and compositions for string orchestra and is an ASCAP Composer Award recipient.

John Fitchuk is a violist who lives in Wheaton, Illinois with his wife Janet. He recently retired after teaching thirty-five years in Illinois, the last twenty-two as director of orchestras at Wheaton North and Wheaton Warrenville South High Schools. He is recipient of the Illinois Outstanding School Orchestra Director presented by ASTA.

Jesús E. Florido, Venezuelan born, classically trained violinist, combines his classical training with his knowledge of Afro-Cuban, jazz, rock, and fiddle music to create a compelling artistry of musical virtuosity and heart. As a highly sought-after teacher, Mr. Florido conducts workshops in North and South America, Asia, and Europe, and teaches annually at the Mark O'Connor Fiddle Camps. He has shared the stage with Zubin Mehta, Pinchas Zukerman, Itzhak Perlman, Whitney Houston, Moody Blues, Robert Plant, and Jimmy Page, and has recorded with Nima & Merge, Healer, Dan Hicks, Gary Hoey, Voyeur, Delarge, Hattler, and Nicholas Gunn. He resides in the Los Angeles area, where he maintains a small private studio.

Robert Gardner is assistant professor of music education at Penn State University, specializing in stringed instrument playing and teaching, alternative styles for string ensembles, and orchestral conducting. He received his undergraduate degree in music education from the Ohio State University, and his master's and Ph.D. degrees in Music Education from the Eastman School of Music. Prior to joining the faculty at Penn State, he served as string instructor for public school districts in Ohio and New York. Gardner was also music director for two youth orchestras at the Hochstein School of Music and has been guest conductor for many honors ensembles.

Jan Garverick is director of four orchestras and AP theory teacher at MacArthur High School, North East ISD, in San Antonio, Texas. A public school music educator for thirty-two years, she was selected by ASTA in 2006 for the Elizabeth Green School Educator Award. Jan is dedicated to the enrichment of life through music and to lifelong learning.

Beth Gilbert, a twenty-five year veteran string teacher, has taught in the Mesa, Arizona Unified School District since 1983. An active music educator, Beth is presently serving on the national ASTA board as a member-at-large. Her orchestra and strolling string groups have performed at numerous AMEA conventions as well as at several national MENC conferences. In 1994 both groups performed at the Mid-West International Band and Orchestra Clinic.

Robert Gillespie, professor of music, is responsible for string teacher training at The Ohio State University, which has one of the largest and most extensive string pedagogy degree programs in the nation. He is immediate past national president of the American String Teachers Association.

Midori Goto is the holder of the Jascha Heifetz Chair and a professor of violin at the Thornton School of Music, University of Southern California, where she teaches private violin, chamber music, and community engagement presentations. Aside from pedagogical work, she also performs more than one hundred concerts worldwide each season, and is committed to numerous community projects that she has founded in the US and Japan, including Midori and Friends, Music Sharing, Total Experience, the Orchestra Residencies Program, University Residencies Program, Partners in Performance, and the Midori Center for Community Engagement at USC.

Karin Hendricks has taught public school orchestra in Utah and Idaho for eleven years. She was named Logan High School "Teacher of the Year" in 2005 and was a 2003 recipient of the US Presidential Scholar Teacher Recognition Award, presented by First Lady Laura Bush. She has degrees from Oberlin College and Brigham Young University and is currently pursuing a Ph.D. in music education at the University of Illinois, where she directs the Illini String Orchestra.

Georgia Hornbacker is associate professor of violin at Millikin University in Decatur, Illinois, associate concertmaster of the Illinois Symphony Orchestra and the Illinois Chamber Orchestra, and is an active recitalist and chamber musician. Ms. Hornbacker attended Indiana University where she received her B.M. and M.M. degrees, studying with Tadeusz Wronski and Franco Gulli. She is a regular reviewer for *American String Teacher* and a contributing author to *Teaching Music Through Performance in Orchestra*. In January 2001, she was awarded the Outstanding Studio Teacher award by the Illinois chapter of the American String Teachers Association.

Kathleen A. Horvath is currently in her sixth year at Case Western Reserve University in Cleveland, Ohio where she is assistant professor of string education/pedagogy and director of the Circle Symphony Orchestra and the Camerata Chamber Orchestra. She also serves as an instructor of double bass at the Cleveland Institute of Music. She is a published in *Applications of Research to String Education*, *String Syllabus*, *Strategies for Teaching Strings and Orchestra*, *Southeastern Journal of Music Education*, *American String Teacher*, *Bass World*, and *Teaching Music Through Performance in Orchestra*.

James Kjelland is associate professor, music education and string pedagogy at Northwestern University in Evanston, Illinois. He received his Ph.D. from the University of Texas at Austin and is a contributing author to: *Teaching Stringed Instruments: A Course of Study*, comprehensive string class method *Strictly Strings*, *The Science and Psychology of Music Performance*, and *Teaching Music Through Performance in Orchestra*. He is author of *Orchestral Bowing: Style & Function* as well as numerous journal articles on string pedagogy in *The American String Teacher*, *The Instrumentalist*, and *Council for Research in Music Education*.

Dottie Ladman is currently an elementary instrumental music teacher for Lincoln Public Schools in Lincoln, Nebraska, and principal violist with the Hastings Symphony Orchestra. After teaching band and vocal music eight years outside of Lincoln, staying home with small children for five years, and substitute teaching for three years, she became a "string specialist" by administrative decree (she could hold a viola so she must be able to teach strings, right?). She is immediate past-president of Nebraska ASTA.

Scott D. Laird, a native of Indiana, Penn., received his B.S. in Music Education and his M.A. in Violin Performance from Indiana University of Pennsylvania. He is on the faculty of The North Carolina School of Science and Mathematics, Durham, North Carolina, where he directs the orchestra, guitar courses, and recording technology programs. He is a National Board-certified teacher, chair-elect of the NCMEA Orchestra Section, and an educational specialist for D'Addario Bowed Strings.

Lori Lauff teaches orchestra at Scullen Middle School in Naperville, Illinois. She completed her Bachelor and Master of Music in Music Education at Northwestern University in Evanston, Illinois, and was recipient of Chicagoland's Outstanding Music Educator Award (2006). She grew up playing viola and violin in South Florida, spent summers at Interlochen Arts Camp, and currently resides with her husband in Naperville.

Dee Martz is the violist on the faculty at the University of Wisconsin Stevens Point, where she serves as director of the American Suzuki Institute, the oldest and largest Suzuki summer school in North America. Mrs. Martz has performed in the Indianapolis Symphony Orchestra, la Orquesta Sinfonica Nacional del Peru, the Indiana String Quartet, and the J.S. Bach

Chamber Orchestra. She was elected to the Suzuki Association of the Americas' Board of Directors in 2001 and to the office of Board Secretary in 2003. A frequent performer and clinician, Dee has presented and performed at many SAA Conferences, and in twenty-five states, Puerto Rico, Canada, Chile, Peru, and Australia.

Joanne May is orchestra director and music department chair at Glenbard East High School in Lombard, Illinois, is a National Board-certified teacher, and currently serves as president of the Illinois Chapter of the American String Teachers Association. She has been named Outstanding School Orchestra Director by Illinois ASTA, is recipient of "Those Who Excel" Award for excellence in teaching, and has been a guest conductor and clinician throughout the Midwest.

Peter Miller resides in Vermont and is currently an orchestra director/string specialist for the Rutland Public Schools. He is an adjunct professor at Castleton State College, as well as music director of the Lakes Region Youth Orchestra. He is a past-president of the National School Orchestra Association, and was recognized in 2004 as the "Vermont Arts Educator of the Year."

Steve Muise is an orchestra teacher and fiddler in Farmington, Maine. He is a graduate of Berklee College of Music, and plays regularly with Maine's premier French-Acadian band "Boréal Tordu" and with his contradance bands Frigate and Muise and Coté. Muise founded the high school multistylistic band the Franklin County Fiddlers, and has performed on multiple recordings and films.

Debra K. Myers is a string specialist for the Fairfax County Public Schools. She is a former president of the Virginia Chapter of the American String Teachers Association and has served as the string representative and secretary of the Virginia Band and Orchestra Directors Association. Mrs. Myers is a frequent guest conductor for district and regional orchestras in Virginia.

Martin Norgaard is the author of the groundbreaking method books *Jazz Fiddle Wizard* and *Jazz Fiddle/Viola/Cello Wizard Jr.* for Mel Bay Publications. His compositions for jazz string orchestra are published by the FJH Music Company. Mr. Norgaard is currently a Doctoral Fellow in Music and Human Learning at the University of Texas at Austin. He is a frequent clinician at state and national conventions such as ASTA, TMEA, CMEA, OMEA, NDMEA, and IAJE. E-mail: martin@jazzfiddlewizard.com, Web: www.JazzFiddleWizard.com

Ray Ostwald directs the orchestras at York Community High School in Elmhurst, Illinois. He also taught in Elgin and Bartlett, Illinois, at the Blue Lake Fine Arts Camp, ISYM at the University of Illinois, and the University of Wisconsin Summer Music Clinic. He has made numerous guest conducting and clinician appearances, and is active as a professional violinist and violist.

Judy Palac is associate professor of music education at the Michigan State University School of Music. She received a Bachelor of Music and a Master of Music from the University of Michigan (Ann Arbor), and a Doctor of Musical Arts from the University of Texas. She is published in the fields of performing arts medicine, string teacher education, and the Suzuki method in such journals as *American String Teacher* and *Medical Problems of Performing Artists*. Palac has held several positions with the American String Teachers Association and is currently national member-at-large.

Bob Phillips, well known as a clinician in this country and overseas, taught orchestra for twenty-seven years prior to his career as a composer and editor for Alfred Publishing. He is known for developing strategies for large-group heterogeneous string instruction that include extensive use of new technologies and for bringing alternative music to the string classroom. He is the author of the *String Explorer, Fiddlers Philharmonic, Jazz Philharmonic,* and *Mariachi Philharmonic* series of books, composer of school performance music, and the founder of the Saline Fiddlers Philharmonic.

Rachel Barton Pine has appeared as violin soloist with many of the world's most prestigious orchestras, including the Chicago, Atlanta, St. Louis, Dallas, Baltimore, Montreal, Vienna, New Zealand, and Iceland Symphonies, and the Philadelphia Orchestra, working with conductors including Charles Dutoit, Zubin Mehta, Erich Leinsdorf, Marin Alsop, Neeme Järvi, and Placido Domingo. Acclaimed collaborations include Daniel Barenboim, Christoph Eschenbach, William Warfield, Christopher O'Riley, and Mark O'Connor. She has been featured on *St. Paul Sunday, Performance Today, From the Top, CBS Sunday Morning,* and NBC's *Today.* She holds top prizes from the J.S. Bach (gold medal), Queen Elisabeth, Paganini, Kreisler, Szigeti, and Montreal international competitions, and has twice been honored as a Chicagoan of the Year. Her discography includes albums for the Cedille, Dorian, and Cacophony labels.

Jack Ranney, former state president for both the Iowa and Illinois chapters of ASTA, recently retired from the School of Music at the University of Illinois at Urbana-Champaign. He currently serves as the conductor of the Parkland Community College Orchestra and is active as a guest conductor/clinician.

Donald Schleicher is director of orchestras and professor of conducting at the University of Illinois and music director and conductor of the Quad City Symphony Orchestra. Previous positions include music director and principal conductor for the opera productions at the Pine Mountain Music Festival, associate director of orchestras and associate director of bands at the University of Michigan, director of bands at the University of Wisconsin-Stevens Point, and band director at Williamsville South High School in Williamsville, New York.

Laurie Scott is director of The University of Texas String Project and assistant professor in the Division of Music and Human Learning at UT Austin. She is co-author of the book *Mastery for Strings: A Longitudinal Sequence of Instruction for School Orchestras, Studio Lessons, and College Methods Courses.*

Phillip W. Serna received the Doctor of Music degree from Northwestern University, where he studied double bass with international soloist DaXun Zhang and Chicago Symphony Orchestra member Michael Hovnanian. He also studied viola da gamba with Newberry Consort founder Mary Springfels. Dr. Serna also holds an M.M. from Northwestern and a B.M. from the San Francisco Conservatory of Music, where he studied double bass with Stephen Tramontozzi. Dr. Serna is principal double bass with the Northbrook Symphony and has performed on double bass, baroque bass, and viola da gamba with numerous Chicago-area and Midwest orchestras. Phillip lives in Plainfield, Illinois with his best friend and wife, Magdalena.

Peter Slowik brings an extensive performance background in solo, chamber music, and orchestral performance to his teaching. Formerly on the faculty of Cleveland Institute of Music and Northwestern University, Mr. Slowik chairs strings and teaches viola at Oberlin Conservatory, while serving as the artistic director of Credo Chamber Music. His students may be found in leading orchestras and university appointments throughout the US.

David W. Sogin is an associate professor of music at the University of Kentucky and serves as coordinator for music education. After receiving degrees from Louisiana State University,

North Texas State University, and UT-Austin, and having taught at every level of string program, Professor Sogin continues to conduct workshops in the local schools and clinics at state and national workshops. He has presented papers on string pedagogy and teaching in Europe, Australia, South Africa, Canada, China, and the United States. Dr. Sogin currently serves on the review board of the International Journal of Music Education.

David Tasgal (M.S., M.M. University of Massachusetts) is author of *The Family String Method* and composer of elementary string orchestra music. He teaches Suzuki violin and cello and school string classes in southern Vermont and northwestern Massachusetts.

Laura Mulligan Thomas has directed the award-winning Charlottesville (Virginia) High School Orchestra for the past twenty-five years. She holds a bachelor's degree in music education from James Madison University and a master's degree in orchestral conducting from Shenandoah Conservatory. A cellist and pianist, Ms. Thomas serves as fine arts chair and editor of the parent newsletter at Charlottesville High School, she is on the executive board of the Virginia Band and Orchestra Directors Association, and she performs with several chamber ensembles, including with her three siblings in the Mulligan String Quartet.

Gwendoline Thornblade was educated at St. Paul's Girls' School in London with an emphasis on viola, violin, and piano. She received a dental degree from London University, and subsequent master's and specialty degrees in Paedodontics from Boston University. She has trained with many renowned Suzuki teachers, including workshops with Dr. Suzuki in Japan. She has taught at Suzuki institutes nationally and internationally, and is a founding member of the Massachusetts Suzuki Association. She is founding director of the Suzuki School of Newton, Mass., and loves playing chamber music and tennis.

Stephanie Trachtenberg received her Bachelor of Music Education from Ithaca College and her Master of Education from the University of Virginia. She is starting her twenty-eighth year of teaching elementary strings for Fairfax County Public Schools in Virginia. She has been a member of ASTA for thirty years. In 1988, she was the first elementary school recipient of the Virginia ASTA State Unit Award for Outstanding Orchestra Program.

Michael Trowbridge received his Bachelor of Music Education and Master of Music in Double Bass Performance from James Madison University. He is in his thirty-first year of teaching, twenty-three years as the director of orchestras at Gar-Field Senior High School in Woodbridge, Virginia. Mr. Trowbridge's orchestras have received superior ratings on grade 6 music every year since 1983 and he has been a finalist for the Agnes Myer Teacher of the Year Award. He has adjudicated orchestra festivals and been a guest conductor throughout Virginia.

Kristin Turner holds a Ph.D. from The Ohio State University where she served as graduate teaching assistant to Dr. Robert Gillespie. At BSU in Muncie, Indiana, where she is primarily responsible for strings/orchestra teacher training, she teaches graduate and undergraduate courses in music education and supervises student teachers. She also serves as director of the Ball State University String Project, coordinates and conducts the East Central Indiana Youth Orchestra, and advises the BSU student ASTA *with* NSOA chapter.

Mary Wagner is the current national ASTA president. She has taught string orchestra (grades 4–12) in the Fairfax County Public Schools for thirty years, where her orchestras have consistently received superior ratings. Wagner has mentored new teachers within FCPS and has been involved in curriculum writing for the county and the Commonwealth of Virginia. Publications include *Getting It Right from the Start* as well as articles in *AST* and *MEJ*.

Effective Practice

Gilda Barston

Practice is a journey. It needs a destination. Frustration occurs when there is no sense of accomplishment. Most students approach practice by repeating a piece over and over with little success. Often they are assigned a set number of repetitions that they dutifully execute. Then they avoid practicing when it appears pointless because they do not see results. Here is a recipe for effective practice.

INGREDIENTS:
Music students who want to improve their playing skills, parents and teachers who want to see their children progress, and students who are ready to assume more independence in their music study.

SERVES:
Music students, teachers, parents, audiences.

1. **Make a plan.**
    Decide what you would like to accomplish. Set goals in very small steps so that you can ensure success. Learning even one measure of a piece is a positive accomplishment, much more productive than trying to learn an entire concerto and ending up frustrated! Isolate just a single problem spot and within that spot, identify the different elements that need addressing. Focus on one point at a time. Think about the left hand, think about the bow, think about the rhythm, think about the tone, think about the intonation, and think about the musical expression. One small spot leads to at least six subspots. Address each separately.

2. **Set a schedule.**
    It is really important to practice consistently. Just a few minutes daily is better than cramming just before your lesson. Set a regular time for practice each day. Everyone's schedule is different. Some students find it most productive to practice in the morning before school. Some like to practice when they get home, before doing homework. Some like to practice just before or after dinner. Once you find a time that suits you, try to keep to your schedule. Remember to practice only on the days you eat.

3. **Structure your practice time.**
    Begin your practice session with a warm-up that focuses on tone and technique and review a favorite piece or two so that you get "in the mood." Next, work on your current piece(s). Work in small sections, with specific goals, and with a one-point focus. Be

realistic; enjoy each step of your progress. Sometimes you won't see immediate results. The time you spend is like putting money in the bank. It will compound and mature at a future time. Remember, Rome was not built in a day!

4. **Avoid pointless or mindless repetition.**

   Practice does not make perfect. Practice makes permanent. PERFECT practice makes perfect! Repetitions that are incorrect just reinforce the mistake. Again, work in very small steps. Be sure that what you are playing is accurate. Practice a very small section slowly to get it perfect, then repeat it slowly. Gradually increase the tempo, being sure that it is absolutely correct in each repetition. If you are repeating a section ten times, only count the good ones. Play "wipe-out:" any incorrect repetition wipes out the previous ones and you start your count again.

5. **Stress quality, not quantity.**

   Teachers are often asked, "How long should I practice?" It is more important to have a productive practice than to have a long practice. Set attainable goals and stop when you have accomplished your goal. The actual time spent at the instrument will vary with the age of the student and the material to be covered. A general rule of thumb is that your daily practice should be at least the length of your lesson time. If you have a 30-minute lesson, do warm-ups for 5 minutes, practice review pieces for 5 minutes, work on your current repertoire for 15 minutes, and spend 5 minutes on sight-reading or previewing new material.

6. **Use technology.**

   Sometimes using a computer program or a piece of high-tech equipment can be fun and useful. Recording or videotaping practice can be an effective tool. Tape small segments of your practice. This will help you evaluate your own playing. Often seeing or hearing what you are doing will pinpoint the practice issues. There are also effective computer programs such as *Smart Music* that can assist in practicing.

7. **Practice technique AND musicianship!**

   Music is about communication. It is an art form that affects our emotions and our listener's emotions. Be sure to include exploring and refining expressive elements (phrasing, dynamics, pacing) in your practice. Do not limit your attention only to skills. Remember, technique exists only to enable you to make music.

Practice is rewarding (and even fun) when it is productive. Remember, there are no difficult pieces. There are just impossible pieces and easy pieces. Practice is the process of making an impossible piece easy. ➤●

Adding a Technological Spice! Using Computer Assisted Instruction for Strings

Susan E. Basalik

"Of course I use technology! I use an electronic tuner and a CD player every day!"

Does the aforementioned statement describe your technology use with your stringed instrument students? Is your computer merely replacing your typewriter and telephone? There are many ways that technologies can be utilized as teaching tools to enhance student learning and performance.

SERVES:
All stringed instrument students and their teachers.

INGREDIENTS:
Buy the best computer that you can afford. Most types of music technology can be used on either a Windows or Mac computer. Check the following when considering a new computer:

- desktop or laptop
- most current operating system: XP (Windows)/OS X (Mac)
- processor type and speed (higher and faster is better)
- size of hard drive (bigger is better)
- monitor size and type (flat screen or CRT)
- sound card and speakers
- USB and Firewire ports
- modem and/or networking
- quality printer

Music hardware. Purchase an electronic keyboard such as a controller (no sound) or a synthesizer (has sound). A USB MIDI device (Roland, M-Audio, Midisport) is needed if your controller or synthesizer does not have an onboard interface.

Other goodies that will enhance you and your students' technology experiences:

- digital camera and/or camcorder
- microphones and cables
- scanner (to enter music for notation programs)
- large external monitor, projector, *Smartboard* if working in a large classroom.

Now add software. Get "smart" and open the box!

Smart Music (Windows and Mac compatible), a program made by Make Music, is a vast collection of accompaniment files for all musicians. Activate the program via the Make Music Web site, then open sound files. Many works including concerti, most of the Suzuki Schools, Essential Elements, and String Explorer are available as *Smart Music* files. Adjust the tempi of the files according to the needs of the student. Attach a microphone to the instrument and computer so that students can play along with the files and receive instant feedback regarding accuracy of their performance. The software costs $100.00, which includes subscription activation for one year and a microphone that can be clipped to the strings between the bridge and the tailpiece. Student home subscriptions are available for $20.00 if the subscriptions are tied to your school or studio account. Visit **www.makemusic.com** for more information about *Smart Music*.

Band in a Box (Windows and Mac) is an excellent and versatile program that allows rapid creation of accompaniment files in a wide variety of styles. *Band in a Box* is easy to learn and use. Simply choose a style, enter the appropriate chords, add a melody, and the file is complete. Files can be easily adjusted for tempo, style, and key. This program is particularly useful with beginning string students as they learn rote songs. "Hot Cross Buns" becomes an entirely different piece when "salsa" is added. Students can use *Band in a Box* as an easy tool for composition. *Band in a Box* ranges in price from $59.00 for a basic version to $250.00 for the "mega" version. Visit **www.pgmusic.com** for more information.

Next Step: Notation!

Using music notation programs can help you with many tasks such as creating exercises, new music, or new arrangements of old favorites. Industry standard programs include *Finale* and *Sibelius*. Both programs allow note entry via computer keyboard or keyboard instrument. Once learned, notation programs become excellent tools for creating and sharing music for both you and your students. Files can be saved as audio (suitable for CD) or MIDI, and Internet file sharing is also possible. *Sibelius* and *Finale* are available in full versions and simple versions. Visit **www.makemusic.com** for information on *Finale* or **www.Sibelius.com** for information on *Sibelius*.

Add Live Action to the Mix!

Live action can include slide shows, video recordings, and/or audio recordings. *PowerPoint* software is an excellent slideshow program that can combine still photographs, texts, and sounds. Create a *PowerPoint* slide show to showcase your program at a school board meeting or create a show demonstrating correct beginning student posture. Banish that "hopscotch hand" by photographing the offensive position for analysis by students. Help students remember that new bowing technique by creating a short video clip, then posting the clip to the Web. Make an audio recording of an excellent lesson or class performance and send it to parents in an MP3 file that can travel via e-mail. Use multipurpose audio programs such as *Sound Forge* or *Peak* for tasks such as audio recording of rehearsals or performances for evaluation.

Mix in Some Fun!

Theory can be made educational and entertaining with software. Younger students can use software such as *Midisaurus*, *Music Ace*, or *Groovy Music* to reinforce concepts of theory, learn about families of instruments, and become budding composers. Older students will enjoy using *Garage Band* and *Acid* to learn about loop generation and composition. Programs such as *Aurelia, Musition,* and *Alfred's Essentials of Music Theory* are good choices for older students to reinforce concepts of theory.

Integrate the Internet!
The Internet continues to expand and become more accessible. There are numerous Web sites that are of assistance to teachers and performers. Find MIDI files from hundreds of composers when visiting the Classical MIDI Archives Web site. Use a legal music file-sharing site to download music. Participate in Web forums to learn how to use software or get advice for questions. *Sibelius,* via a plug-in known as *Scorch,* allows creation of files that can be sent via Internet that can be viewed and heard by the recipient exactly how the file was composed. Students can e-mail recorded *Smart Music* files to their teachers for assessment. Take advantage of what the Internet can offer you and your students.

Yields:
Adding technology to your teaching mix can yield outstanding results for you and your students. Your creativity as a teacher will increase and your students will benefit. Remember: **Technology is enhancement, not replacement!** ➤●

Blur and Focus Your Way In (Tune)

Louis Bergonzi

SETUP:

Teacher:	Someone in the orchestra is out of tune. Please fix it. *(Students smile back and sustain the out-of-tune pitch.)*
Teacher:	Okay, the problem is in the lower strings. *(Cellos and basses smile back and sustain the (out-of-tune) pitch.)*
Teacher:	Okay, cellos it's you. Alone and fix it, please. *(Cellos smile and sustain the same sounds they have been doing all along.)* Come on. You tell me. Is that in tune? *(Students look back at teacher.)*
A Student:	*(with a mixture of certainty and doubt)* No. *(The student strongly suspects that "No" is the correct answer because of the nature of teacher's question and tone of voice; Nonetheless, it's still a 50/50 risk the students have learned to take.)*
Teacher:	Good, right *(with a feeling that at least s/he has taught them something this year)*. It's not in tune. One of you is out. *(Students smile back and wait for the teacher to either tell them who it is or to "go down the line" in order for the teacher to figure it out. They know that if the teacher does go down the line, they'll be told who it is and probably which way to move fingers. So they wait.)*
Teacher:	*(looking at clock to see how much time is left in order to decide whether to go down the line or just tell the basses)* Ok, here's what we're going to do . . .

INGREDIENTS:
- A single sour pitch that has been sustained in the oven too long and won't bake into something that's pleasant to the ear.
- String players, or wind players, who are sure that they are among the ones playing a pitch in tune and that it must their neighbor or someone else who is wrong.
- One or two hands, provided by teacher.
- A teacher who can hear the difference between in and out of tune and wants her/his students to learn to do so as part of their musical training.

SERVES:
Orchestra students, their teachers, and their audiences.

Basic

1. The ensemble, or a subsection thereof, holds a single pitch.
2. Teacher waves flat hand up and down as a signal for players to "bend pitch" up and down[1] as follows:
   a. Strings players: by moving the finger used to produce the pitch in question.
   b. Wind players: by adjusting embouchure and/or wind speed.[2]
   c. Timpanists: by adjusting pedal.
   d. Percussionists or everyone: vocally.
3. Only when the initially out-of-tune pitch has been sufficiently disassembled by the blurring does the teacher change her/his flat waving hand into a still, closed fist. The fist is a signal to stop blurring the pitch and to "focus" into the correct sound.
4. Students then focus their blurred pitch to the correct one by listening to the group consensus and blending in. This process of listening and adjusting is what they thought they were doing before (see ingredient 2), but weren't.
5. Teacher should re-blur a focused in tune pitch, even—and especially—when it is correct. (See "Caution" below.)

Variation: Double Recipe Using Left and Right Hands

First, follow the above recipe to get a part of the orchestra to be in tune. The basic should be a familiar routine before trying this variation.

1. Teacher divides orchestra or subgroup into two: Group A and B; assigns each group to watch and follow a particular hand (left or right).
2. Following the teacher's closed fist, Group A sustains the in-tune pitch as the reference goal to which Group B is going to focus and tune.
3. Group B blurs pitch according to hand signal given by the teacher's other hand.
4. Upon teacher's signal, Group B focuses their blurred pitch in order to be in tune with the audible correct pitch that the other group is sustaining for their benefit.
5. Teacher can control who is blurring and who is focusing by changing hand signals shown by each hand.

Option:

Recipe can be used with intervals or chords as long as there is an aural reference against which the players can gauge their own "in-tune-ness."

Caution:

The teacher should never indicate to students whether their focused note is in tune or not. This defeats the goal of putting the students in charge of their intonation accuracy. Instead, the teacher should re-blur the pitch until it settles correctly. Also, the teacher should frequently re-blur even an in-tune pitch in order to 1) provide a repetition, and 2) to ward off complacency on the part of the students, who will quickly assume that whenever the teacher stops blurring, they must be correct and therefore they can stop listening.

Notes

1 The width of the blur/bend is up to the teacher. I suggest that the blur be proportional to the degree of the out-of-tuneness of the initial attempt at playing in tune. For example, if players are painfully out of tune, then have a wide blur.

2 Younger trombonists may move slide instead of adjusting embouchure.

Non-String Players Teaching Strings: A Recipe for Success

Jeffrey S. Bishop

INGREDIENTS:
A music teacher (instrumental or vocal) with a strong desire to teach strings

SERVES:
The entire orchestra community through the preparation of highly qualified teachers.

The American String Teachers Association with the National School Orchestra Association has predicted that there may be a shortage of 5,000 qualified orchestra teachers in the next generation of music educators. With demand for string programs growing, it is imperative that all qualified music teachers—regardless of their background—feel that they can become successful string teachers. Anyone with a strong desire to teach strings, coupled with the drive to learn the technical side of the pedagogy, can and will become a competent, if not successful, orchestra director.

I have concentrated this recipe on teaching the beginning level of strings. I strongly suggest studying privately on an instrument as you teach beginning classes—learning along with your students is an excellent method of teaching as well!

Bowing Terms
Non-string players are often intimidated by the various terms for bowing. This is unfounded, as any good musician knows how to articulate, regardless of whether he or she is singing or playing an instrument. The easiest way I've found in my career to relate band or choral teacher to string teacher is to equate the use of breath to the use of the bow. In band and choir, air is the medium by which the music is articulated. The bow is the articulator in string playing. Terms such as *legato*, *staccato*, and various other articulations are synonymous in application if not in name. Yes, there are specific French and/or Italian words for these bowings, but the same general effect can be achieved often times by simply singing the articulation to the string players. There are several good resources out there for specifics (see below), but the articulations break down to two basic ideas: Bow on the String (*detaché*), Bow off the String (*spiccato*). Remember: it is the amount of SPACE BETWEEN the notes that determines the exact bowing.

Beginning String Classes
The best thing about teaching beginners on string instruments is the fact that you can see everything! The posture is easily identifiable and the correct playing positions can be seen and corrected, if needed, immediately. The hand positions can be assessed easily as well. I

find that if you get them set up correctly from the very first class session, you will have fewer problems down the road.

For violin and viola, the student should sit on the edge of the chair with the feet flat on the floor, shoulder width apart. I like to have the students start without the instrument and play a little game. I tell them that I should be able to pull or push them out of their chair so that they will stand up without any problems. I then walk around the room shaking hands and randomly pulling students to their feet. Yes, it's goofy, but the students think it's fun and it gets my point across.

The instrument is placed on the left shoulder. A correctly fitted shoulder rest should be used to support the space between the student's neck and the instrument. The jaw is allowed to rest on the chin rest while the left hand is brought up to the neck of the instrument. The left hand should never squeeze the neck of the instrument. If fit properly, the combination of shoulder rest, chin rest, and instrument should set comfortably with the student. The scroll of the instrument is turned toward the music stand, twisting at the torso slightly to accomplish this.

For the cellists I like to start the same way, with the feet evenly spread, but then I do things a little differently. The endpin should be extended so that the scroll of the instrument is eye-level when the student stands. As the student sits, he or she widens the stance to the left slightly, allowing the cello to rest against the left leg a little more than the right. This will help line up the instrument along the center of the body while keeping the C peg behind the left ear. The left hand forms a "C" shape (I tell the student to imagine holding a can of soda) and rests on the fingerboard, the thumb on the neck below the second finger.

For the bass players, you'll have to decide whether you want them to sit or stand. If sitting, the proper stool and instrument combination is essential. I start my students standing, as it is a little easier, I find, to get the proper posture. The endpin should be adjusted so that the nut of the fingerboard is about forehead level (this varies greatly with the size of the student–just try to avoid having the student reaching up for half-position) with the bass in front of the student. The bass is pulled back toward the student while keeping a slight forward lean to the instrument. The weight of the bass is used to help the student set her fingers "into" the strings. The left hand forms the letter "C" like the cellists, and the arm is brought up into first position. For the bassists, it is essential that the left elbow not be allowed to drop, collapsing the wrist and twisting the hand position. While this is true for all string instruments, it is critical for the bass players, as the size of the instrument can quickly lead to more physical problems.

So what about the bow?

The bow hold–notice I used the term "hold," not "grip" (a picky distinction, yes, but one that can subliminally cause tension in the bow hand and arm)–is basically the same for the violin and viola: the thumb is curved, allowing for a hollow hand, up to the bow stick while the first three fingers are placed over the top of the stick, the second finger lying over the dot on the frog. The fourth finger perches on top of the bow stick near the screw. As the students progress through bow exercises, they quickly discover that the pinky finger is there to counterbalance the weight of the bow.

For the cello and bass, I have the student open the right hand palm up with the fingers spread open (have the students visual putting gum balls between their fingers). The bow is placed on the right hand so that the stick lies across the first knuckle crease on the first and fourth fingers. The thumb curves up to the bow stick just in front of the frog. Keeping the rounded, hollow shape produced by the curved thumb, have the student turn their hand over—voilà! Instant bow hold! (I do not teach German bow hold for the basses.)

Once the posture has been perfected, the teacher can move onto more musical matters. Selecting a text for the string class should be done the summer before the class begins. There are several wonderful texts available now; some even come with CDs and DVDs so the kids can hear and see lessons. Choose one with which you can feel comfortable and familiarize yourself with it. Reading through the teacher's edition of these textbooks can alleviate many of your concerns.

For the first two years of study, technique will be emphasized utilizing the textbook series chosen. Supplementing the texts with literature will be the next step. Many of the textbooks will have correlated literature that is published separately. There are also many great pieces that have been listed on the MENC Orchestra Super List (www.menc.org). If you have a required state music list, purchase a copy for your school. If you don't have one, try to get your hands on the Texas UIL Required Music List. This is one of the best lists out there and has graded literature for beginners through high school.

As you program for your concerts, never forget that you are educating your audience as well as your students. In the first year of study, take time during the performances to do demonstrations, explaining how things work. Parents who understand the concepts that you are teaching are more apt to support their students. Parents who are involved will also encourage students to practice and take private lessons.

Middle School and High School String Classes
When I first started teaching string classes I was paranoid that I had to know everything. I frantically tried to absorb as much information as I could but quickly learned that it was impossible to know it all. It will never fail that some student will throw you a curveball in a rehearsal—one of those questions you have absolutely no idea how to answer. Just tell them, "I don't know, but I'll find out and tell you tomorrow." Then go call a colleague or look it up. It's okay! You will have students who can play their instrument better than you can—and BRAVO to you for it. That means you're doing a great job. But never forget that you're the professional educator. You'll always have something to offer your students.

With middle school orchestra, it's important to keep going strong on technique. The urge will be to put more emphasis on performances, as there will undoubtedly be more of them at this level, but try to maintain a good balance between technique and literature. Etudes can be assigned from books designed for the instrument. Vibrato should also be introduced. If you don't feel comfortable with it yourself, there are good books out there on the subject, and at least one textbook designed for the middle school orchestra (*Viva, Vibrato!* published by Neil A. Kjos Music Company).

High school orchestra presents the opportunity for more performances (concerts, contests, trips), but you will need to maintain the balance of technique vs. literature. I know I keep coming back to this, but it's an integral part of my teaching style. I honestly believe that the time invested in technique (scales, etudes, vibrato, shifting, etc.) is time later saved in rehearsals learning literature.

Getting Started
The opportunities for teaching orchestra are out there. Right now, somewhere in this country, there is a school orchestra program that does not have a qualified orchestra teacher in

charge of it. This is inexcusable. The students are suffering because of it. If you are interested in getting started down the path of string education, I suggest that you spend some time during the summer at a teacher's resource workshop. There are several on the ASTA Web site: www.astaweb.com. Spend time talking with colleagues who teach orchestra. Attend new literature reading sessions. Do everything possible to make yourself the finest string teacher possible. ➤●

Forming the Cello Left Hand

Muriel Bodley

INGREDIENTS:
String students who have good cello posture and are able to use the bow fairly well

SERVES:
Cellists of all ages.

Teacher is seated in *front* of the student

1. Model a good left hand position.
2. Let student feel the shape of the teacher's hand on the fingerboard.
3. In seated position, without the cello, have student drop one hand at a time from above the head to the knee, letting each hand fall freely so the student feels the weight of the arm.
4. With cello: Several times drop the left hand from the height of the head to the fingerboard near the bridge.
5. Slide the hand on the D string back to 4th position, where you have put a piece of moleskin (Dr. Scholl's) for the thumb—starting in 4th position sets the arm level.
6. Stand the first, second, and third fingers tall (**mountain peaks**), first finger mountain peak points BACK to the pegs.
7. Thumb is relaxed and fingers are firm.
8. Slide the whole hand slowly back to 1st position and STOP when the thumb hits the bump, half of a large Dr. Scholl's corn pad taped on, so the thumb ends up opposite the second finger.
9. Student places the third and fourth fingers on the finger tapes. Teacher pulls the first finger into position so it is leaning on the back side of the finger tip. Student does NOT TURN AROUND and look at the first finger.
10. After a few times of repeating the exercise, have the student PUSH the first finger slightly back when other fingers are set. *Do not look at the first finger; just move it back.* (Almost all young cellists play their first finger sharp.)
11. Tap each finger and thumb 10 times.
12. Be sure the thumb is:
    a. not too far under the neck; make a bunny cave between the cello neck and palm of hand
    b. placed on the corner (not FLAT)
    c. parallel to the bridge
13. Use a mirror!

I have this little rap that students repeat after setting the hand. They get a big kick out of it and it seems to make a point. It's easy to find a rhythm to it:

Mountain peaks, mountain peaks

Pull first back,

Thumb hits the bump,

And keep it soft,

Bird wing up,

Wrist is flat.

●

Jump Start Your Beginners!

Judy Weigert Bossuat

Put the children's enthusiasm to work for you! Make simulated instruments and take advantage of the 10–20 days that it takes for parents to obtain rental instruments or the district to complete the eligibility paperwork for loaned instruments.

INGREDIENTS:
Excited new beginning string players awaiting rental/distribution of instruments.

Violins and violas: Empty cake mix boxes stuffed with crumpled newspaper. Paint mixing sticks from the local hardware store glued and taped on to simulate the fingerboard.

Cellos: ¾" PVC pipe, a cross-joint in order to attach the two short pieces that will fit inside the knees, 4 ends to finish off the ends of the pipe, a 4" section of larger pipe taped where the bow would play and large enough in diameter to accommodate the real bow.

Bows: ½" or ¾" dowels cut to the appropriate length, an eraser or domino taped near one end to simulate the frog.

Foot chart of some sort: paper squares, carpet, pizza circles, open file folders.

SERVES:
Elementary beginning students and teachers looking for ideas to start the year.

Advantages:
Simulated instruments make the first few classes silent while establishing good posture, bow hold, and key words: "rest position," "playing position," "ready–play," etc. Class routine and discipline can be set without the distraction of instruments replete with various sounds just waiting to be discovered!

Drawing a foot chart helps control posture while giving the teacher an easy way to take roll and control the children's placement in the room.

Collect the real instruments while the students are using the simulated ones and use non-class time to place finger and bow tapes, check bridges, add rubber bands, and shoulder sponges.

Have the children "earn" the real bow and then "earn" their real instrument, once basic playing position, rhythms, and left hand position and function have been established.

When the class puts the bow on the real instrument for the first time, the position and sound are good, and parents and family members are forever grateful. There is initial muscular control so the children can focus more attention on good tone and intonation.

Recipe:
1. Draw the foot chart—rest position feet and playing position feet. Add the student's name. Make an extra one for home practice.
2. Establish instrument position and the ability to get from rest position to playing position and the reverse.
3. Establish bow hold. Do bow movement exercises (up/down, circles, etc.)
4. Hold the stick bow and pretend instrument at the same time.
5. Learn to play rhythms and simulate changing strings. Practice playing on command, keeping the bow direction correct (up/down/angle with the instrument). Note: Placing violin/viola bows where the box intersects with the stick neck helps establish straight bowing.
6. Place the left hand. Learn correct hand position and practice proper finger placement. Use dots or stickers on the paint mixing stick and PVC pipe necks to indicate pitches.
7. Learn scale and simple piece fingerings. Provide accompaniment and the melodic relationship to finger movement with a piano or violin/viola/cello.
8. Replace the stick bow with the real bow and repeat all the steps on the pretend instrument.
9. Graduate to real instruments.
10. Continue the progression with the real instrument. ➡

The Nutritionally Balanced Private Music Studio

Mimi Butler

As a studio teacher, follow this recipe for a successful studio and you will be professional and organized.

INGREDIENTS:
A bright, uncluttered studio
Targeted marketing
Professional looking invoices
Aggressively set lesson fees
Pre-interviewed students and parents
Entertaining recitals
Parental involvement

SERVES:
Private studio teachers in a home or rental location.

1. **Select an appropriate location.**
   This location must have parking, appropriate lighting, space, and a bathroom facility.

2. **Weigh lesson fees.**
   Talk to other private studio teachers in your area. You can even inquire about fees for college preparation exam tutors or school tutors. Your fee needs to be competitive: not too high and not too low. If you choose to travel to teach, add the travel fee onto the lesson fee. If you rent a location, your fee must cover all rental costs.

3. **Preheat your marketing strategy.**
   Create business cards and a brochure. This can be accomplished on the computer. Contact school teachers and other private studio teachers with a letter and a phone call. Send them business cards and brochures and ask them to put you on their private studio teacher list.

4. **Bill the parents of your students in monthly or semester size portions.**
   You can offer discounts for those students paying by the semester or school year. Create bills on your computer using QuickBooks. Include a letter or newsletter with a monthly bill. Charge a nominal late fee if the bill is not paid by the 15th of the month.

5. **Measure your income and deductions.**
   QuickBooks is the best way to keep track of all income and deductions. You can declare a portion of your home monthly bills for your studio along with studio and office supplies, music supplies, convention costs, business expenses, and much more. Don't forget to hire an accountant each year to do your taxes.

6. **Select ripe prospects—the initial interview.**
   Before you sign a student up for lessons in your studio, set up an initial interview with the student and parent. Go over your policy sheet and listen to the student for a few minutes.

7. **Work on your presentation.**
   At least once a year you should have a student recital. Make sure you charge a yearly recital fee or activity fee to cover all expenses.

8. **Add side dishes to your private lessons.**
   You can offer group lessons once a month, master classes, summer music camp, holiday music camp, home school classes. Don't forget to charge for monthly classes the same price as a weekly lesson fee.

9. **Season to your parents' and students' tastes.**
   Create a simple Web site to communicate with parents. Include schedules, announcements, studio information, concert information, and even pictures. Send a newsletter or regular e-mails to the parents and your students.

A Recipe for Cello Left Hand/Arm Placement Success

Tanya Lesinsky Carey

This recipe is adapted from the teaching recipes of Margaret Rowell and Irene Sharp and is completely explored in *Cello Playing is Easy: Part 1, Warm-Ups* by Tanya L. Carey. Balance and flexibility are the special ingredients that make this construction versatile. This recipe is unusual in that it does not use the thumb as an anchor.

The secret to making this recipe is to follow the directions step by step. Experience each step with awareness and understanding before proceeding to the next. First impressions are lasting.

SHOPPING LIST:
Small sticker dots to mark finger placement:
- Place a sticker between the D and G string opposite the G on the D string.
- Place a second dot between the D and G string opposite the E on the D string.

Tennis ball
Toy car or miniature skateboard
Coat hanger
Cello

INGREDIENTS:
One weighted arm
4 fingers to support the weight of the arm
2 ears to hear pitch
5 parts balance
5 parts flexibility
1 connected body—essential to success
2 smiling faces
Peripheral vision to "see" fingers
Generous portions of patience and time

SERVES:
This recipe feeds the performer ease and confidence in motion, the listener beautiful pitch, and the observer free balanced motion. It is low in calories because it is *easy* and uses minimal effort.

Preparation:
1. To prepare forearm muscles:
   - Thumb flips with each finger (finger over thumb nail). This is an isometric exercise.

- Water flick with each finger (thumb over finger).
- Knocking the weight of the arm/loose fist along the length of the fingerboard.

2. To prepare feeling of arm weight and placement:
   - Place the tennis ball on the strings and slide it up and down the fingerboard with your arm/hand.
   - Put your fingertips on the long side of a coat hanger like a string. Have your partner hold the hook. Pull back and forth to feel your arm/back muscles work.
   - Rest your fingertips/hand/arm on a miniature skateboard or toy car. Slide the car/skateboard up and down the fingerboard with your arm.
   - Place your fingers on the fingerboard. Slide your arm/hand/fingers up and down the fingerboard as though the fingertips were wheels.
   - Pulling *slightly* to the left on the string with curved fingers, slide the arm down the string as though you still had the ball in your hand. Lift the structure off at the end of the string so you hear a strong ringing sound. Continue the follow-through action *over* the bridge as though you are throwing the sound to someone. The arm is angled so that you can read an analog wristwatch or see a sticker on the wrist.

Construction of the Balanced Arm/Hand/Fingers

- Depress the D string at the G♯ on the D string with the RIGHT hand.
- Balance the left arm on the D string on the dot marking G by placing the fourth finger at 1 o'clock on the roundness of the string–not at 12 o'clock pressing down, not at 3 o'clock on the side of the string.
- Pull the arm slightly outwards. The other fingers are on the string also with little weight.
- Pluck the fourth finger G several times in a rhythm.
- Lift 4 and pluck the third finger F♯ several times in a rhythm.
- Slide the first finger back as far as it will go on the string (the explorer finger) and return it to the rest of the hand/fingers a few times. This easily establishes the open hand shape from the start.
- Pull the first finger back a little bit to the E dot.
- Lift fingers 2 and 3 and pluck the first several times in a rhythm.
- Raise the arm so the "C" for cello hand-shape contacts the neck with the thumb.

Things to Watch for During Construction

- The arm weight is always on the string unless the thumb "marks the place" while the fingers are off the strings.
- The thumb is the open string finger.
- The chest is the counterbalance for the arm weight. Pull back with the arm and feel this–stable end pin, please.
- The left knee counterbalances the pull to the left by the arm.
- If the thumb is to contact the neck, it is placed *after* the arm weight feeling is established. The contact point is more often on the *side* of the neck, not the middle of the back opposite the middle fingers. If a marker is used, the thumb bumps up against it from below with a side contact point, not placed on the bump.
- Placing the thumb first and then the fingers immediately teaches the muscles that the thumb is the most important and causes grabbing.
- For variety in exploring minimum effort, tape a plastic straw to the side of the neck of the cello. Play with the thumb on the straw without collapsing or bending the straw.

Mastering the Recipe for Memorization

Christina Castelli

"Whoops! I think you just looped back to the beginning of the piece. Did you forget the transition to the next part? Oh, I see . . . some of these passages sound the same and you're having trouble memorizing them. Have you looked at this piece lately?"

INGREDIENTS:
Determined string player, recording of the piece, metronome, dedicated teacher.

SERVES:
String students, teachers, and audiences.

1. **Isolate the problem.**
   Locate the passage that is difficult for your student to memorize.

2. **Listen to the passage.**
   Ask your student to listen to that passage on a recording numerous times, focusing on the rhythm as well as the line of the notes and whether it ascends or descends in pitch.

3. **Eliminate technical challenges.**
   Guide your student in practicing any technically challenging phrases. Your student should begin by playing each phrase slowly, addressing the technical problem associated with each one. Once the technical challenges are overcome, the phrases can gradually be brought up to tempo with the help of a metronome.

4. **Eliminate mental challenges.**
   Help your student resolve confusion over fingerings and bowings. Clarify fingerings and bowings wherever necessary, or consider opting for an alternate fingering or bowing that may work better or fall more naturally for your student. Encourage your student to slowly practice the phrases containing these confusing fingerings and bowings, gradually increasing the tempo.

5. **Link challenging phrases with the passage.**
   Once your student has mastered a technically or mentally challenging portion of the passage, he should move one phrase before and one phrase after the section, and begin to incorporate the challenging section into the rest of the passage.

6. **Play through the entire passage.**
   Once your student has mastered the stumbling-block sections (the ones that present the greatest challenges for them), have your student play through the passage in its

entirety without stopping. If your student becomes stuck on a phrase, isolate that phrase and practice it out of context several times until it is solidified. This process should continue until the student is able to successfully play through the section without stopping.

7. **Play it again and again.**

   The student should not be complacent and assume that one successful play-through of a difficult passage is, in and of itself, a recipe for certain victory over the passage. It is important to successfully play through the passage numerous times without stopping. It is equally important to continue to isolate the difficult phrases within the passage to ensure that the student's facility increases over time.

8. **Link the entire passage with the rest of the piece.**

   Once your student can successfully play through the passage, it needs to be linked with the rest of the piece. This can be accomplished by gradually working backwards, adding larger and larger phrases onto the ends of the passage until the beginning and ending are incorporated, or it can be achieved by starting at the beginning of the work and joining each successive passage to the previous one. Working through this linking process over a period of days or weeks will enable students to eliminate or downplay the stigma associated with the difficult passages in the piece, helping them make a smooth transition from one passage to another within the piece.

9. **Reinforce memorization.**

   In order to reinforce memorization of passages, your student should devote a portion of her practice time each day to playing through the piece. Retention of meticulously practiced passages can be lost within an hour if not reinforced through repetition. Encourage your student to strengthen the connection between the difficult passages and the rest of the piece by successfully playing through the entire piece at least once (without stopping) at the end of the practice session each day, noting any passages that gave her pause.

Memorization is a great hurdle for many music students and is compounded for string students because of the additional effort required to master bowings and intonation, as well as fingerings. While slow practice is always a key step in learning any passage, careful analysis of the specific technical or mental challenges encountered in memorization problems is essential and is a significant part of the solution. Encourage your students to listen carefully not only to recordings but also to their own playing, and to bring patience and determination to every practice session. With those tools and your expertise and your support, your students will master the recipe for memorization in no time! ➥

Ten Tasty Treats to Set Up a Natural Bow Arm

Lisa Cridge

SERVES:

All string players, especially beginning violinists and violists.

INGREDIENTS:

1 gingerbread musician in great position to support the instrument and bow

A spine that feels long and shoulders that are soft can help a musician correctly hold his or her instrument and bow. (The image of gingerbread will remind the student that their muscles will feel pliable and lengthened, but not rigid.)

Game: Have the student hold the instrument in playing position with a body that feels soft like freshly baked gingerbread. Have them inhale and exhale.

1 boiled egg thumb

Boiled eggs have a rounded feel without being hard, even if they're hard-boiled! ☺

Thumbs of great players bend, flex, and roll as the player's bow travels from frog to tip.

Game: Have the gingerbread girl or boy wave "hi" to another student with their boiled egg thumb. They will become aware of the thumb's importance and make new friends, too. Have them notice how the thumb can feel rubbery, like a boiled egg!

1 donut "o" and one donut "hole"

The circle between the thumb and middle fingers can be compared to the shape of a plain donut. The soft space found between the thumb and second finger can be likened to the hole of a donut. Students should feel this circular shape in their hand since it serves as the fulcrum or central balance point in the hand. Great tone depends on the balance found in this circle.

Game: Have students create a circle with their right thumb and second fingers. Have them look through the circle. Then they can swing their arms to some music, keeping the circle. When the music stops, they can check their donut circle and look through the hole!

4 cookie dough fingers

The bow hand fingers will curve naturally around the stick and feel heavy and relaxed like heavy cookie dough.

Game: Have the young musician "plop" their doughy fingers around the bow stick. The teacher can hold and support the weight of the bow at the frog and at the tip so the student can experience "dead weight"—the heavy cookie dough feel. Teachers can give students a "ride" while the students' fingers are in position. The fingers may jiggle a bit, but should not fall off!

4 ice cream knuckles

As the bow fingers find their places on the stick, they can immediately feel slightly melted.

Game: Have the student make a "too-tight" frozen ice cream bow hold and then melt the grip until the bow *nearly* falls. Play this game sitting on the floor, just in case the bow really slips. This may be a good time to have a conversation about the cost of a bow . . .

1 gummy worm first finger

The first finger can be slightly separated from the other fingers to balance the hold. Often, the first finger grabs too tightly. Draw a line on the part of the first finger that will rest on the stick.

Game: Make a bow hold and pretend that the first finger is a gummy worm. The middle fingers can be "worms down in the ground." Pretend that the first finger worm is softly slithering down the stick a bit to see what is "down the road."

1 marshmallow palm

Great tone comes from hands that are soft enough to transmit energy from the imagination, into the arm, the fingers, and strings.

Game: Have the student play a piece of music and the teacher can guess if the player's palm feels like a marshmallow. Even if the teacher does not guess the correct answer, the student has become more aware of the way his or her hand feels.

1 cooked macaroni pinky

It is crucial to teach beginners to curve the fourth finger, especially when they play at the frog.

Game: Without the instrument, have the student place the bow's tip on their left shoulder. Have them lift the bow in the air and place their curved bow thumbs on their left shoulder. Their little fourth finger will be soft and curved like *cooked* macaroni. Their bow can hop back and forth, touching their shoulders with either the tip or frog. Have the students focus on the "frog" bow hold when their curved thumbs are on their shoulders. Ask the kids if their macaroni is cooked!

1 cup of oil (canola or olive oil for good health)

Drizzle "oil" in a student's elbow and wrist. The bow will move "out" and parallel to the bridge.

Game: Without bow, place left palm on right arm, near the elbow. Move the right hand down to the wrist and back, in a "polishing" motion. The teacher can "drip some oil" in the right elbow so the student can see how the right forearm opens and closes like a door hinge.

If students bow "crookedly," they can try playing near a wall so that the upper arm is forced to stay relatively still while the forearm opens and closes. Teachers can check to see that the student's instrument is placed well, since it can appear that a child is bowing incorrectly when in actuality, the instrument may not be aligned correctly with the body.

1 salt-water taffy road

The bow can travel parallel to the bridge with an image of a road. The student can pull the bow on the "sticky" road. This image can help avoid a "slipping" bow and an unfocused sound.

Game: See how many bows the student can play while *watching* the bow with his or her eyes. If the student can focus on this game, he or she has great concentration!

Game: Have the youngster close her eyes and see if she can *hear* if the bow is staying on the road. How many singing tones can the student make with a "straight" bow? ➤●

Choosing Ensemble Repertoire: A Recipe for Success or a Recipe for Disaster!

Winifred W. Crock

One of the most important jobs of a music director or conductor is choosing an ensemble's repertoire. It is crucial to choose engaging programs that the ensemble can play beautifully in the given amount of rehearsal time. The repertoire should be educationally appropriate and of the best musical quality. Meeting these goals is a huge challenge. So, consider the following . . .

Serve the Best
Choose the best music possible. Try to select unedited masterworks whenever possible, but you must consider the technical and musical abilities of your ensemble. Fortunately, there are many easier, quality arrangements that are true to the composer's concept. There are also many excellent newer works. Be particular about your choices.

Many Play the Notes, Few Play the Music
Don't pick repertoire that is too difficult for your students. If they have to work too hard to play the notes, they may not be able to play the music. Most ensemble repertoire should be easier than the average solo ability of the players.

Offer a Balanced Program
Balance the technical and musical demands of a given program. Alternate technically difficult works with easier pieces that contrast musically as well. A balanced program will allow immediate study of musical interpretation and ensemble techniques. An ensemble will mature more easily with this approach. Consider a musical appetizer to open a concert: a short, easy work that will allow the ensemble to "warm up" in public. What about a fun, fast piece at the end as a programmed encore or "dessert?"

Use Authentic Ingredients
Consider ensemble size, balance, and instrumentation when choosing repertoire. While it is not always feasible to perform repertoire exactly as the composer intended, aspire to historically correct performances whenever possible. For example, do not program a Mozart symphony with the 350-member all-district orchestra or choose a baroque concerto grosso with fourteen basses in the section.

Variety Is the Spice!
Vary period, style, and tempo in music selections. Avoid an evening of "Adagio in D major." Contrast makes listening more interesting and playing more fun. Themed concerts—a

baroque evening, an all-fiddle concert—can be lovely, but carefully program contrast into these occasions as well. Variety of key, meter, tempo, style, and size of ensemble are all points to remember.

Offer Appealing Selections But . . .
Programming music students love can be great motivation, but don't choose repertoire just because you like it, or because they like it, or because you have always wanted to conduct it.

Increase the Menu
Hopefully your ensemble will love the repertoire you have chosen, but if your ensemble clamors for something else, remember: people like what they know. Influence and broaden what your students know by playing recordings often, especially before they see the music. The "a-ha!" factor of recognition is a very positive force. Talk about why you like the music and why it is important for musicians to learn it. If they still want to play something else, offer a selection or two of their choice for "dessert."

Ask Students to Try New Things Many Times Before Passing Judgment
Our musical tastes change with age and experience. Often students don't like a work because they cannot play it or they do not yet musically comprehend it. Ask ensemble members to reserve repertoire judgments until they can play it well. If they still don't like it when they have mastered it, then respect their opinion.

Program to Your Ensemble's Abilities
Consider your group's strengths and weaknesses. "If you have a big gun, shoot it!" "If you have an amazing dish, serve it!" Program the "William Tell Overture" if your trumpets and solo cellist are stellar, but avoid the "Overture to the Barber of Seville" with a beginner oboist. If you are not sure that a particular section or featured soloist can play a piece, pass out the music in advance to those students and hear it before everyone else begins to work on the piece. Do not assume they will "get it by the concert." Get to know your ensemble before you make the final concert selections.

Timing Is of the Essence
Carefully consider the amount of rehearsal time available for preparation. Choose music that will allow at least half of the rehearsals to focus on musical interpretation and ensemble techniques. Don't fall into the trap of selecting very difficult repertoire thinking there is plenty of time for refinement. Is your ensemble mature enough to deal with the same difficult repertoire for an extended period of time? Would easier selections and more frequent performances be a better option? Rarely does the "sight reading in public" feeling or the "beat this one into the ground" concept produce meaningful musical experiences.

Consider a Timely Change in the Menu
If things are not progressing as you had hoped, be willing to alter your program. A last-minute repertoire change is usually not productive, but don't be afraid to make a switch early in concert preparation.

Not All Repertoire Needs to Be Performed . . .
Some dishes, especially new recipes, are best served to family! For variety in rehearsal, sight-read repertoire in a variety of styles and play easier pieces that focus on one or two technical

points. Rehearse some repertoire that nourishes your group's skills of balance, blend, tone color, and dynamic contrast. Finally, play some music just for fun! Performance repertoire may evolve from any of these categories, but also may be different music entirely.

Choose carefully, play musically, and enjoy! You will serve a musical feast! ━●

Chinrests and Shoulder Pads: Finding the Proper Fit

Patricia D'Ercole

INGREDIENTS:
Students who have tension in their left shoulder, arm, or hand *or* students who have posture problems
Various assorted styles and heights of chinrests
Various assorted styles and heights of shoulder pads

SERVES:
Any number of upper string players who wish to play in a more relaxed, healthy, and comfortable manner.

Step 1
Fit the student with the proper height chinrest first (not the shoulder pad).

Follow this principle: The space between the collarbone and the jaw should be filled in by the chinrest plus the thickness of the violin or viola.

When assessing the fitting, check the following:

- The student's hand should be in playing position on the neck of the instrument or resting on the bow shoulder so that the left shoulder assumes the same position as when playing. Do NOT let the left hand hang at the side of the body.
- The instrument should be balanced on the collarbone and trapezius muscle (the large cord at the top of the shoulder).
- The head should come down to the instrument resting on the shoulder and collarbone, not the shoulder up to the chin.
- When looking at the student from the back, the student's head should lean slightly to the left, less than 45 degrees from center.
- The jawbone, not the chin, rests along the edge of the chinrest, so that the student's neck is not thrust forward and the muscles on the right side of the neck do not protrude.

Recipe substitutions:
- If the head leans too far to the left, a higher chinrest is needed. Layers of cork can be added between the chinrest and the instrument. (Shoe inserts made of cork can be obtained from your local shoe store.)
- If the height seems correct, but the chinrest is uncomfortable, try a more shallow cup. For a temporary fix, cut a small oval of Dr. Scholl's Mole Foam only enough

to cover about 50 percent of the cup area and place in the center of the cup, leaving the edge exposed. If the chinrest is still too deep, cut a second larger piece of mole foam that will extend closer to the edge of the chinrest and place it over the first layer. Do not cover the edge of the chinrest, as the jawbone must be able to catch the edge of the cup like an interlocking piece.

- Husky children sometimes need the Flesch chinrest with the cup centered over the tailpiece. This puts the instrument further back on the shoulder and makes it possible for them to bring their arm under the instrument without undue strain.

Step 2:

Follow this principle: The shoulder pad should fill in the space between the back of the violin and the relaxed shoulder when the left hand is in playing position.

- A shoulder pad that is too high will cause the instrument to be lifted off of the collarbone, thus causing the player to lose contact with the instrument. In this instance, the head can also tilt back or to the right.
- A shoulder pad that is too low causes the shoulder to elevate, which will restrict the left hand, especially for vibrato and shifting.
- Check that the curve of the shoulder pad is actually over the shoulder. With Kun shoulder pads, this can be remedied by moving the left "foot" of the shoulder pad to the notch closest to the center and then moving the right "foot" further to the right to fit the instrument.
- Clothing worn for performance should be taken into account when fitting a shoulder pad. For example, those wearing tuxedo jackets may need a thinner instrument shoulder pad if the shoulder pads of the jacket are thick.
- Especially young players who have no space between the back of their instruments and their shoulder should have a thin layer of foam (1/4 in.) or a chamois to provide some traction and to keep the violin/viola from slipping on their clothing.

Remember that once a student is properly fitted with the chinrest and shoulder pad, comfort is not guaranteed forever. Body parts grow in different proportions and at different times so that, especially during the teen years, this issue may need to be addressed again. ➤

A Recipe for Developing a Core String Tone: "Wheaties for Students with a Wimpy Sound"

Andrew H. Dabczynski

INGREDIENTS:
Any string player—with at least elementary technique and sound-producing abilities—who displays an undernourished, weak, "surface" string sound, or those of any level ready to develop a deeper "core" string tone and/or more substantive bow/string contact.

SERVES:
All students looking for a richer, deeper tone.

1. **Establish a baseline aural model.**
    Instruct students to listen intently to their sound as they play any tune (e.g., a simple method book melody, scale pattern, etude, etc.) representative of their technical level.

2. **Discover arm weight.**
    After setting down their bows, instruct half of the students to allow their right arms to fall limply by their sides—as if their arms are asleep. The other half of the students become "practice buddies." Each practice buddy will then gently lift the "sleeping" arm of his/her partner to shoulder height, holding the limp appendage out at arm's length! The student with the "sleeping" arm should be careful not to help the buddy by using any of his own muscles to support the arm; the buddy should be doing all the work! After 30 seconds or so, the practice buddies will begin to discover that the arm is, of itself, a relatively heavy body part! Reverse roles so each student makes this discovery! The point: the arm is plenty heavy; we don't need any extra pressure to make a big string sound.

3. **Use the "dagger" bow hold.**
    After picking up the bow again, every student changes the proper bow hold position to the "dagger" bow hold. Students hold their bows like daggers or clubs, with the palm facing inward—each student should see his/her own palm. This is essentially the same as a very sloppy bass German bow grip!

4. **Discover the natural spring of the bow.**
    Instruct students to place their bows—using the dagger grip—on the D string at approximately the spot of the bow's balance point. Without making any sound, students then pull down into the string, causing the string to flex, and setting the spring of the bow so the stick of the bow meets the hair. Draw attention to the "chin-up" action of the muscles (as opposed to a "pull-up" muscle action), and the weight of the arm as it "collects" in the elbow. Allow each student to release the spring of the bow (without

30

making any sound!) by relaxing the arm. Repeat the process—reset and release the bow spring—a few times.

5. **Discover maximum bow/string contact.**
Still using the dagger grip, students set the spring of the bow once again, allowing their arm weight to pull down through the string, so the stick of the bow meets the hair, and the hair of the bow has maximum string contact. Now instruct students to maintain the arm weight and "sticky" string contact while they move the D string back and forth *without making a sound!* (A few telltale "grunts" of the bow will likely be heard at this point.). Now count, "1, 2, 3!" and on "3," have all the students play an open D while they maintain maximum, super-sticky string contact through their pulling arm weight. The sound will be an awful, grunting, grinding sound, but it will represent *total* maximum string contact and core tone! After calming down the group (!) instruct the students that they are never allowed to make that sound in public again!

6. **Discover the concept of "pulling" arm weight versus "pushing" arm pressure.**
Instruct the students to return to their correct, perfect hand position. (Phew!) Repeat the process of discovering the natural spring of the bow, this time using correct bow hold. Be sure the students can feel the arm *weight* as it "collects" in a moderately lowered right elbow. Teachers should then have students differentiate this experience with the feeling of a *raised* elbow that presses downward, instead of one that pulls.

7. **Discover the collé stroke:**
Again encourage students to experiment with establishing "sticky" bow contact on the string, moving the string silently back and forth as the stick meets the hair (as in step 5, above), only this time maintaining a correct bow hold and arm weight (*not* pressure!) through a lowered elbow. Instruct the students—all together now—to set the spring of the bow and lean as if they were about to play an up-bow stroke. But instead of moving the bow laterally, instruct the students to release the sticky bow/string contact *vertically*, so the bow "pops" out of the string. Conduct the students to release the bow on the count of 3, so there is a collective "pop" sound upon the release. This is a rudimentary collé bow stroke. Reset the spring of the bow and repeat the process, this time having the students lean as if they're going to play a down-bow. Reset the repeat the basic *collé* stroke in both directions until the strokes have a consistent "pop" at the beginning of each stroke.

8. **Extend the collé stroke to a core tone.**
Instruct students to set the spring of the bow (as in step 7, above), and lean as if they were going to play another "popping" up-bow *collé* stroke. But this time, instruct students to move the bow laterally, after releasing the initial "pop." As they do so, they should continue to feel the weight of the bow focused in the right elbow, and a sticky string contact should also be maintained. Repeat the process, this time leaning down-bow. After consistency of sound and motion is established on separate bow stokes, alternate up- and down-bows, being sure to allow time between each stroke to set the spring of the bow and to concentrate focus on the sticky bow contact.

9. **Rebuild the aural model.**
Lead students in playing again the initial tune/exercise performed in step 1, drawing attention to the new, deeper, richer "core" tone that has replaced the previous superficial, surface tone. Encourage students to recognize and describe the new sound—and to seek the core sound in both *forte* and *piano* contexts.

10. **Extra portions.**

    Repeat recipe on a daily basis for a week or two. Revisit regularly, being sure to add extra rosin powder as necessary! Add the sugar and spice of dynamics over a full plate of fine repertoire!

11. **Enjoy feasting on a healthy sound!**

    Never again fear that your students will play with an undernourished, wimpy tone! ➤●

Conducting: A Recipe to Increase the Yield of Your Rehearsal Time

Sandra Dackow

Double and Triple the Output of Your Rehearsals!

INGREDIENTS:
Elementary or middle school string students, conductor podium, chairs, stands, pencils, broadcast (not visual) tuning machine, wastebasket, and a teacher who visualizes himself/herself as a conductor.

SERVES:
The greater good (orchestra students, teachers, parents, and the music).

YIELDS:
Double or triple the results of any other approach.

1. Room is equipped with chairs and stands set up as an orchestra for students and a podium for the teacher. Any remaining chewing gum is filed in the wastebasket before instruments are unpacked. Each student has a pencil, *under pain of death*.

2. Generate an A from the tuning machine. Everyone listens without moving or making a sound. After 3 or 4 long seconds, nod and have students match their A strings to the tuner. Repeat for each string. Give a low E to the basses separately from the violin E. While this is happening, there is no talking, no playing/practicing/noodling, and no plucking of any kind—absolutely zero tolerance. Students are very appreciative when this atmosphere is established and enforced, as it enables them to double or triple the output of each rehearsal.

3. **Act like a conductor** as you teach in rehearsal.

   a. Stand on the podium. (You are easier to see and you can control the environment.)
   b. Use a baton. (You are easier to see and this forces you to develop your own good technique.)
   c. Keep your own pencil at the ready, as a good example.
   d. Know your score, regardless of the level of the music. Don't learn the music along with the students—you will not be able to make effective use of either eye contact or time management otherwise. Analyze and mark even the easiest scores—your students will respect your ability to improve their yield through your own preparation.
   e. One sheep dog can control an entire herd of sheep by using eye contact. Directives accompanied by eye contact yield a higher rate of compliance than verbal directives alone. Know your scores and look at the players.

f. Keep the room focused and the pace fast; no one even has time to be distracted if the pacing is effective. *Turn up the heat.* If you use your hands and eyes to control the room, you will not need to ever raise your voice.

g. Insist that everyone use pencils both defensively (avoid repeating mistakes) as well as offensively (write in ideas to make the music more beautiful). Good players use pencils constantly in rehearsal.

h. Insist that no one plays any note unless it is in response to one of your conducting gestures. This can't be stressed enough. If you don't conduct it, they should not play it. *This will solve nearly every problem and add years to your life.* It will increase your rehearsal output tenfold or more. Believe in yourself and your ability to lead from the podium.

i. Have students match attacks, weight, dynamics, and bow speed to your gestures. Your output will increase beyond your wildest expectations once you establish a cause-and-effect relationship between what the students see and the sound they produce. Your baton should govern their bows and the sounds that they produce. You are powerful enough to have the orchestra under fingertip control if you believe in yourself.

j. Teach the group to produce a huge sound before scaling back to softer dynamics. Show, with your gestures, different combinations of bow speed and traction.

k. Conduct the same way you would a fine orchestra. There should be no difference in your approach. Give one prep beat. If you are clear, there is no need for extra beats (or a whole bar); never count off or use an audible breath as a prep. Students will follow whatever is logical and clear. We create problems when we give audible preps or too many prep beats—this teaches them not to actually trust or respond to good conducting. Giving extra beats or redundant verbal instructions are not necessary ingredients and are as pointless as adding pepperoni to oatmeal. *When students tune out the conductor, it is a recipe for disaster.*

l. Realize and understand that *YOU are the real variable*, not the students. They will sound as well as you conduct. To get them to sound better than your conducting, you will need more time to make up for this inefficiency.

4. Word will spread. Be prepared for invitations to guest conduct and present clinics. Everyone wants to get more bang for their buck; the chef who can pull thirty-six blueberry muffins from a recipe and ingredients meant for six will be greatly in demand. ➡

Recipe for Violin/Viola/Cello Instrument Sizing

Jean Dexter

Why penalize your students with an instrument that is too big, when you, yourself, may play on an instrument that (according to the usual measurement procedure) may be too small? When changing from one size to another, it is best to aim for the middle of the range, erring on the side of too small rather than too large. This is best for the ease of playing and comfort of the child.

INGREDIENTS:
Yard stick (with or without instrument size indications)
List of real instrument measurements or actual instruments of varying sizes
Willingness to set aside old thoughts

SERVES:
Violin, viola, and cello students.

Violin/viola students:
1. Measure the length of the outstretched left arm from the neck to the WRIST.
2. Choose an instrument with that length from tail button to top of scroll. This will allow for a 90-degree angle of the left arm.
3. Measure the width of the left shoulder. Check this measurement with the length from the tail button to the first rib corner. This will allow the shoulder to better support the violin.

Cello students:
(more complicated without an actual instrument due to varying body parts affected)

Basic Measurements
1. Have the student sit tall on the edge of a chair.
2. Have the student bend down the head so you can find the "VP" bone (that protruding bone at the top of the spine/base of the neck).

   • Measure from the chair seat to the "VP" bone.
   • Measure the length of the student's arm from the shoulder to the base knuckles.
   • Measure the length of the student's thigh from mid-hip to the center of the knee joint (while sitting).

Consult the chart below to help with the appropriate cello size:

Cello Size - Suzuki	Cello Size - European	Height in Chair	VP Bone	Thigh	Bow Arm	Back of Cello
1/10	1/16	Under 24"	Under 15"	Under 9"	10"–14"	15"–17"
1/8	1/10	24"–26"	15"–18"	9"–10"	11"–16"	17"–19"
1/4	1/8	26"–28"	17"–19"	10"–14"	12"–18"	21"–23.5"
1/2	1/4	27"–31"	19"–22"	12"–15"	16"–21"	23.5"–26.75"
3/4	1/2–3/4	30"–34"	22"–24"	14"–17"	18"–25"	26.75"–28"
Full Size	Full size	34" and higher	24" and higher	16" and more	25" and longer	28" and more

How to Instill Enthusiasm in the Lethargic Orchestra Member

Joanne Donnellan

INGREDIENTS:
A high school (or middle school) orchestra class containing one or more lethargic members
A piece of music the orchestra can play quite well

SERVES:
The entire orchestra.

Background for this Recipe
Like the spice that sits hidden behind the more flamboyant spices in the cupboard, the lethargic orchestra member often tries to hide behind his stand, near the back, feeling inadequate among other players, wanting to join in, yet at the same time hoping to not be noticed.

Method:

STEP 1
During rehearsal call the lethargic student up to stand next to the podium and be the "listening ears." His job will be to listen while the orchestra plays a passage or an entire piece, then give them feedback on what he has heard. Being called upon and trusted by the teacher to give comments will give him/her credibility among his peers, and the teacher will undoubtedly be amazed at what the lethargic member hears musically and can verbalize to the orchestra. He will undoubtedly "tell it like it is," which will amaze the rest of the orchestra. They, in turn, will try to correct whatever it is he hears that needs to change.

The orchestra members will focus and work! They will also enjoy this fresh input!

The process can be repeated with this student, or he/she can choose another student to stand next to the podium and be the next set of "listening ears."

Added ingredients: you could call on the same student(s) or different students three or four days in a row especially if you are doing final preparation for a concert or festival performance.

STEP 2 (On another day!)
When a piece is 90 percent learned and the teacher has difficulty motivating the students to put the final touches on phrasing and dynamics for a polished performance, call upon the lethargic student to come to the podium and "direct" the orchestra in playing this piece through the use of pantomime—acting out what he wants the music to say, rather than actu-

ally conducting. Orchestra members will respond with interest and clarity in their playing. They will watch him because they will be curious to see what he'll do. This attention in turn will motivate the lethargic student to be more creative and a little more "crazy" in his use of pantomime, especially as he begins to feel response to his actions from the orchestra.

Try this on a piece the students are comfortable playing—suggestions would be a Hungarian Dance by Brahms, a Slavonic Dance by Dvorak, Beethoven's *5th Symphony*, or any other piece that has drama and mood changes.

Students love this and it can really wake up a sleepy rehearsal! The lethargic student will also be energized when he returns to his seat and will contribute more to the group. He will actually become excited about the music!

Notes

I have often chosen a student who outwardly seemed less musically aware than most other students in the orchestra and have been surprised at what he/she could hear and verbalize to the group. Often the quietest student is one of the best at pantomime!

It is important the teacher creates a comfortable "you can do no wrong" atmosphere in the classroom in order to make this recipe work. Use this recipe sparingly; once or twice a week is enough, and not every week!

Rehearsals need variety and the spice of creativity to keep students motivated. This recipe, in two parts, works beautifully toward that end! Enjoy! ➟

A Robust Cake to Nourish You and Your String Program

Ian Edlund

Partake freely of this *before* and *during* your visits to the "smorgasbord" of teaching "entrées"—techniques, methods, materials, and parent meetings.

INGREDIENTS:
Basic playing and teaching skills
Desire
Determination
An open mind

SERVES:
The best interests of teachers, and thereby students of all ages and abilities.

The Base Layer
The **foundation** has to be strong and secure. It could benefit from the liberal addition of sweets and nuts. Be a solid, competent player and keep active as a performer whether as a soloist, an orchestra player, or a chamber musician. Make your performing *visible* to your students and their parents by promoting your musical activities as well as the other offerings of your community. It's important that your students realize the importance of musical participation in your life.

The Second Layer
Maintain and improve your **professional involvement**. Be an active member of your professional organizations, such as MENC and ASTA. The contributions you make by working in these organizations will return to you many times over.

The Third Layer
Continuing education. Keep on learning. Take some lessons, maybe on a secondary instrument. If you teach full orchestra even occasionally, study clarinet and French horn. Attend summer string teachers' workshops and your state MEA conference regularly.

The Fourth Layer
Communicate with your colleagues. It's important that we support others who "speak the same language." Find out when their concerts are, then attend as many as you can. What you

will learn will amaze you . . . Your colleagues will appreciate your support and perhaps return the favor. Organize a regularly scheduled quarterly "gab-fest" of string teachers in your area to share ideas and war stories.

The Icing

Hold all this together and decorate it with the most important part: **the icing**. Whip together a large batch of eager students, a never-ending stream of contagious enthusiasm, and a seasoning of empathy and humor. Color it by experiencing music of varied styles and origins. Apply the icing heavily enough to enrich the cake without overpowering the subtleties in the textures and flavors of the layers. ➡●

Antidote for Violin and Viola "Tip Specialists"

Teri Einfeldt

INGREDIENTS:
1 student who avoids playing in the lower quarter of the bow
1 persistent teacher
1 fresh cake of rosin
1 violin or viola
1 bow
The name of the student's best friend
1 one-octave scale of your choice

SERVES:
Violin and viola students and their teachers.

Step A.
- Approach the student carefully—you may get injured by the flailing frog!
- Check the bow to ensure there is indeed rosin on the bottom quarter.
- Encourage the student to form her most useful and well-thought-out bow hold/balance.
- Adjust as necessary. Have the student reciprocate and adjust your bow hold/balance that you have purposely set incorrectly.
- Challenge the student to recreate the model that you molded on her own hand.
- Have the student place the bow at the frog on the A string, close to the pointer finger on the right hand. Call this spot (close to the pointer finger) the "house" in which the student's friend lives.
- Check for roundness in the bow hand, curved pinkie with two bumps, bent thumb, raised elbow that slopes gently down from the right knuckles, and non-rotated forearm. Bow hair could be turned a fraction towards the bridge, depending on taste.
- Ask the student to play a one-octave scale concentrating on returning to the friend's "house" on every up-bow. Tell the student that at the end of every up-bow she has to report whether or not she has arrived at her friend's "house."
- Choose a passage from a previously learned piece and try to apply the same concept.

May take several weeks to gel!

Step B.
- Have the student form his best bow hold/balance but move it up approximately 2 inches closer to the tip so that the pinkie is just above the winding of the bow.
- Have the student play a one-octave scale and on every up-bow he must hit the "clip" (ferrule) of the bow traveling off the string beyond his hand.
- After successfully completing this task, try again without hitting the "clip" but go as close as possible.
- Choose a passage from a previously learned piece and try to apply the same concept.

May take several weeks to gel!

Step C.
- Instruct the student to play one short note at the frog, lift bow off the string, and play another short note at the tip.
- Alternate between the two ends of the bow without moving the scroll of the instrument.
- The fingers and thumb must be bent when playing the note at the frog.
- Again while at the frog check for roundness in the bow hand, curved pinkie with two bumps, bent thumb, raised elbow that slopes gently down from the right knuckles, and non-rotated forearm. Bow hair could be turned a fraction towards the bridge, depending on taste.
- Choose "Perpetual Motion" by Suzuki or an alternate piece or scale and continue the same exercise.

Step D.
- Invite the student to play a one-octave scale with all whole-bow up-bows. Begin each note at the tip and end each note by moving the bow hand around the head without touching their own hair with the bow. Circle back to the tip, set the bow firmly against the bow hair, wait to settle in, and feel the natural weight of the arm. Repeat throughout.

Students who do not play at the frog are uncomfortable getting to the frog. Things to stay on top of to improve comfort ability include: bent thumb, elbow that is somewhat elevated but still gently slopes down from the top of the hand, rounded bow hand that does not include a straight, locked pinkie, and a non-rotated forearm.

Work on this at every lesson for at least two months. ━●

Recipe for an Open-Fingered Handwich

Gerald Fischbach

INGREDIENTS & MIXING INSTRUCTIONS:
- Dynamically balanced left arm, hand, and fingers (Dynamic Balance: Balance in Motion)
- The elbow lane is a No-Parking Zone! The left elbow swings to accommodate a change of position, string, and finger.

SERVES:
All string players with a taste for a relaxed, balanced, authoritative left hand.

Violin/Viola
The left elbow swings in towards the belly button for:

- change to lower string
- change to higher position
- change to higher finger

The elbow swings out to the left for the reverse of the above.

Cello/Bass
The left elbow hangs closer to body for:

- change to higher string
- change to lower position
- change to lower finger

The elbow swings out away from the body for reverse of the above.

Left Arm-Hand-Finger Alignment: Keep the Geometry Simple
Keep these ingredients in a fairly straight line, with only gentle bends:

- elbow
- wrist
- base knuckles
- middle joint of middle finger

Avoid wrist kinks of four varieties (in, out, left, right); all are undesirable ingredients.

Violin/Viola: Avoid outward bend of wrist in lower positions; keep bend to a minimum in higher positions.

Open the Hand Back
- Drop the left hand and fingers into the fingerboard by releasing some of the weight of the arm.
- **Violin/Viola** start with third finger; **Cello/Bass** start with fourth finger.
- "Open the hand back" for in-tune spacing of the fingers.

Happy Fingers
- Strike and release, not strike and squeeze.
- Find the "sweet spot:" place the finger back on the fleshy pad, a little to the thumb side of center.
- Balance the hand and arm on the finger in use.
- Rule of Finger: Only one finger down at a time (this rule can be broken on occasion)!
- Fingernails: short (required), painted with pretty flowers (optional).

Rule of Thumb
- The Rule of Thumb: There Is No Rule of Thumb!
- Where does the thumb go? Where does the 800-lb. gorilla sit? Anywhere it wants to!
- Tap the thumb to find its happiest spot in any given situation.
- As with the elbow, the thumb adjusts to the finger, string, and position in use.
- In lower positions, the violin/viola thumb tends to locate opposite first finger, the cello/bass thumb under second finger.
- The thumb addresses the instrument neck on the inside edge of its pad, not flat-on, in the center of the pad.

Mix and balance the various ingredients above for a lifetime of tasteful string-playing enjoyment! ➞

Tips for Recruiting Beginning Orchestra Students (Or, "How to Get All of Them")

Kathy L. Fishburn

We all know that recruiting always comes at the very worst time of the school year. But, it is our future and with some preplanning, everything will fall into place.

INGREDIENTS:
Elementary-aged students who have never played a string instrument
Elementary school teachers, principals, parents
A string teacher who needs recruiting ideas

SERVES:
Students who don't know what they're missing.
Parents who may or may not know anything about music.
Teachers who are looking for a good "crop" of students.
Schools and communities that are in for a treat.

1. **Before the actual recruitment time frame:**
   Make yourself an integral part of the school by attending all kinds of functions throughout the school year. It is so important for all the parents to know who you are. Take time to make friends with the other faculty members and keep your principal informed about the progress of your orchestra program. Make your beginners visible to the school's younger students. Contact your local music store for any help they can give you. If possible, take a look at the standardized test scores of the students to be recruited.

2. **Long-range planning is essential for success.**
   Arrange a time for a concert/recruitment program. Try to select music that the children will understand and appreciate. Make sure it sounds great! Give all the students a letter explaining the program at your school and ask that they return the bottom portion of the letter (name, address, etc.) to their homeroom teachers. Alert the teachers and principal that the letters will be coming back. Prepare an upbeat presentation and assemble all the handout information and other gimmicks.

3. **Recruiting.**
   At the end of this recipe is a recruitment letter that I have found to be most successful. The returnable bottom portion of the letter is the necessary information that you will need for mail-outs or phone calls. When doing the actual recruitment, use a demonstration group of students that the children will recognize from their school. Select a

few students to try out the instruments with the help of the performers. Make repeated visits to the student's homeroom and make sure that all the forms are returned. Back up your visits with phone calls to the parents. Follow up by providing lists of new students to the principal and teachers for next year's planning. Send a letter to the new parents about the requirements for next fall.

Dear Parents,

Your child has been selected for the most wonderful opportunity. He/she has been invited to become a member of the Bivins Elementary Orchestra. The beginning orchestra meets every Tuesday, Wednesday, and Thursday during the school day. No advance musical training is required. The students will start at the very beginning, learning how to hold the instruments and to read music. The Bivins Orchestra will offer your child the experience of learning to play a musical instrument, learning to read music, and the joy of working with and performing with a group of students. The instruction will continue into middle school and high school. It is proven that children in music score better on the SAT and ACT tests when in high school. This is an extremely important decision for you and your family because this is the only time in the child's education that beginning orchestra will be offered.

The school provides all the music lessons. However, each student will need his or her own instruments. All the music stores have a rental purchase plan. This way, you can rent the instrument, to make sure that your child enjoys playing before you have to purchase the instrument. The music dealers carry the instruments that I have recommended. If you already have an instrument, please allow me to take a look at it to see if any repairs need to be made before the next school year begins. If you plan to purchase an instrument, please make sure that it is European made. This will help ensure the quality. I want all the students to get the best start possible.

If you have any questions or problems, please do not hesitate to call me. I look forward to many years of working with you and your child.

Sincerely,

Ms. Kathy L. Fishburn
468-9442 home
kathyfishburn@arn.net

(Please return the bottom portion of this letter to the homeroom teacher.)

NAME _____ TEACHER_____

ADDRESS_____ PHONE_____

ZIP _____SCHOOL NEXT YEAR_____

INSTRUMENT YOU WANT TO PLAY _____

PARENT SIGNATURE _____

A Recipe for Confidence

John Fitchuk

INGREDIENTS:
1 or more musicians lacking in confidence, vintage unimportant
1 or more challenging musical passages, carefully selected
Patience, liberally applied

SERVES:
Any and all who desire more confidence in their playing.

As an adjudicator, this scenario has been repeated on more than a few occasions: the performance begins and I am impressed. Everything is in place: tone, rhythm, accuracy, style, vitality, etc. This could be the finalist! At some point, though, the performance begins to deteriorate. The confidence and energy dissipate. Now, like a long-distance runner, the goal is just to cross the finish line. My comment begins, "If you had just finished like you began . . . "

Confidence is everything in performance. I sometimes feel there is an invisible barrier between the stage and the audience. As performers, it is our confidence that breaches that barrier and allows us to create this rapport between performer and listener. How do we develop this confidence?

I use this analogy with my students. When I am driving to a destination for the first time, I am apprehensive. I keep glancing at the directions that I have written down. Is this the third street and I turn right or was that the gas station that I needed to turn left at? We feel comfortable when we know where are going.

It is no different in performance. The performer needs to be confident of the destination. To accomplish this, I practice backwards. I reverse the process of how we normally learn a piece. Whether it is the end of the piece or a difficult passage, I establish the destination and then begin the process of working backwards. It could be by groups of sixteenth notes or small phrases. I keep adding notes or phrases to my repetitions until the passage is thoroughly learned. Throughout the process, I am reinforcing the destination and, in turn, my confidence of arriving there.

I have used this process with ensembles as well, with the results always being successful. A desired benefit was that the students would add this technique to their individual practice. Nothing guarantees a successful performance but proper preparation and the confidence that accompanies it is certainly an important ingredient. ➡

Improvisation: It Tastes Good!

Jesús E. Florido

A recipe for those who want to be free of the page and play what is really inside of them.

INGREDIENTS:
A warm functioning body, a creative brain, two good ears, one of your favorite tunes, an adventurous spirit, your instrument, some fingers, two full arms, a splash of sweat, and SPICES!

SERVES:
All string students looking for a way to express themselves and become better musicians.

1. **Pick a tune.**

   Any tune will work, but it is very important that it be a tune you like. It can be from any musical source, including the radio or recordings. For your first tune, one that is not crowded with many instruments and parts will be best. This will allow you to hear yourself better. Please start simply. As you gain experience, the sky will be the limit.

2. **Add your ears to the mix.**

   Listen to the tune and memorize it. Be able to sing it without your instrument first, and once you can sing it back in your head, learn to play it on your instrument like you sing it. Go slowly at first, and then speed it up. Take your time!

3. **Add your own "personal" rhythms.**

   Start to change the rhythm without losing the melody. For instance, subdivide the notes into half of their value so you can groove. Groove is where you place the rhythms in relation to the beat in any given phrase. Are yours on the front or back of the beat? You will not be able to groove until you can play on the center of the beat with a metronome. (The metronome will set you free!)

   Find a common note (the tonic is always a safe bet) that you think will work, and start to find your way around the melody by playing other notes your ears think can fit it. Another good way to try the melody is to play it but leave some notes out. Silence is music too. Remember, you don't have to play all the time during a solo.

4. **Add the spices.**

   After you have all the wholesome ingredients, mix them together and add spices (see below). About 80 percent of them are located in the spice rack of your bow, but don't be afraid to experiment. You never know what you might find in your left hand.

The spice rack includes accents, tremolo, ricochet, flying staccato, etc. On the left hand rack, experiment with glissandos, vibrato speed, and the four leading fingers.

5. **Shake it, shake it, shake it!**

   In a single bowl (solo) or a bigger dish (a jam with your friends), shake it all together until it grooves to a great taste.

For further culinary experimentation, choose other tunes, or even make one up yourself.

Remember, diversity is the cure for boredom. ➤●

Step Up to the Buffet: Alternative Styles Stew

Robert Gardner

This is a traditional recipe that can vary greatly depending on who is preparing it. It has been around longer than most people realize, and has often included bowed string instruments at various times in the past. Don't be shy about using new technology in the preparation of improvised dishes based on contemporary trends. Learning to perform new styles of music is a great way to cultivate your students' developing palettes with new flavors and textures.

INGREDIENTS:

String student musicians with an appetite for developing their creativity

Any of a wide variety of musical styles (including but limited to: old time fiddle, jazz, maria-chi, Celtic, blues, or rock)

Orchestra teachers interested in expanding their musicianship and making new friends

SERVES:

As many as the rehearsal space will hold.

1. **Musicians always learn to perform within the context of a genre, and can be proficient in multiple styles.**
   Students should have the opportunity to taste (perform) a variety of musical styles, even using amplified or electric instruments when possible.

2. **Integrated curriculum reform is the key for flexibility and potential for success.**
   Allow students to view concepts and issues from perspectives different than their own through music making in styles with which they were previously unfamiliar.

3. **Performances should always represent the musical genres as authentically as possible.**
   Collaborate with local musicians who are fluent in a particular genre (bowed string players when possible, but others also welcomed). Let their expert knowledge of the performance practices of the genre guide the preparation of respectfully authentic performances.

4. **Plan lessons that allow for sharing ideas about music making, so that all participants learn from each other within an exploratory atmosphere.**
   Teachers learn about new musical genres along with the students, and the guest performers learn about the children and the educational process. The guest artists will probably be pleasantly surprised by the students' interest and enthusiasm, as well as how quickly they learn to perform the music.

5. **Classical musicians gather to "rehearse," but garage band musicians call it "jamming."**
   In fact, "jamming" is a universal term that includes playing music in any context, and it is sometimes used in a friendly invitational manner (e.g., "We should get together and jam sometime"). The creative process in garage bands, which can be a good model for lessons, is usually more democratic than in a traditional school ensemble. Opportunities to jam provide chances to utilize new skills and can inspire a need for more practice.

6. **The worst that can happen is that they say no.**
   Don't be afraid to invite the best-known musicians in your area to perform and work with your students, because they can inspire community interest in your program. Artists enjoy performing and discussing their music with new people, and are sometimes willing to work for modest stipends for such opportunities.

7. **More can be better.**
   Developing musicality within the context of a different genre does not happen at the expense of previously developed skills. In other words, learning to play blues violin doesn't make you a worse classical player. In fact, learning to use instrumental executive skills in a new way can inspire interest, expand musicality, and even develop a deeper understanding of classical technique.

8. **Pick good tunes.**
   As in any setting, the repertoire you choose greatly influences the curriculum that will be taught. Once you've selected a genre, choose pieces that are representative of the styles of tunes commonly performed. For example, if you were performing Irish music, you might choose to play an air, a reel, a hornpipe, and a jig. The best pieces are the ones that the expert players of the style are probably the most tired of performing. Use recordings in lessons, and encourage your students to seek out other recorded music for listening.

9. **Leave them wanting more.**
   Encourage students to seek other ways to develop their skills in multiple genres, such as taking private lessons with local musicians, attending concerts, listening to recorded music, practicing with play-along recordings or computer programs, and attending jam sessions at local establishments.

I hope that you will share this recipe with your students, and that they will enjoy learning to perform new styles in an open and exploratory atmosphere. Shared musical experiences help students to become a part of a community of creative musicians. These experiences can, in turn, influence the musical participation of generations to come.

Successful Social Activities for Orchestra Students

Jan Garverick

Social as defined by Webster: *marked by pleasant companionship with one's friends; tending to form cooperative and interdependent relationships with one's fellows.* Using Webster's definition as a guideline, the author will describe several social events. The first five activities are the favorite traditions of the MacArthur Orchestra students.

INGREDIENTS:
String students who unite in common social purpose to learn more about each other and music

SERVES:
All orchestra members in a particular school, plus chaperones.

Recipes of Tried-and-True Social Activities

1. **Evening Concerts of the San Antonio Symphony.** At least four times a year, we attend the symphony concerts as a group. Students board the bus at school at 7:00 p.m. A local law firm provides a grant for high school groups: $1.00 per person for the Friday night symphony ticket; students pay $4.00 for the round-trip bus for a grand total of $5.00 per student for a delightful evening. Taking two buses (88 students), we return to school at approximately 10:30 p.m.

2. **Annual Opera Study.** Group trip to either Austin Lyric Opera in Austin, Dallas Opera in Dallas, or the Houston Grand Opera in Houston. An elegant evening, including dinner. Travel is by charter bus. We attend the pre-concert lecture at 7:00 p.m. and take a backstage tour, if possible, afterwards. Students discuss the specific opera libretto and listen to the music two months ahead. English subtitles run above the stage. This is the fusion of all arts—music, dance, drama, light and set design, costumes, creating a total arts experience. Cost runs about $50.00 per student for discounted opera ticket and bus, payable in two payments of $25.00 each. We usually take 55 students. Cost is more if the trip is overnight. I am always amazed at how much the students enjoy this activity. Operas we have seen recently are *The Marriage of Figaro, The Magic Flute, Rigoletto, Cosi Fan Tutte, I Pagliacci, Cavalleria Rusticana, Der Rosenkavalier, Norma, Carmen, The Barber of Seville,* and *Don Giovanni.*

3. **Hauntcert.** This is a string fest (a Halloween theme) with our cluster middle school and elementaries on a Saturday morning before October 31st. High school students arrive at 10:30 in order to teach the 5th graders the sound effects for a student-composed ghost story. Each high schooler works with three or four 5th graders (teaching

sound effects), then we rehearse the story together with the narrator. The elementary students also rehearse several prepared open-string songs. Meanwhile, the middle school orchestra rehearses on stage. All wear their school shirts and nice jeans/tennis shoes. 11:30 a.m. is concert time for all orchestra students. Format equals open-string songs by 5th graders, scary songs played by the middle school orchestra, and two suitable selections by the high school students, including the sound effects story with 5th graders. The 30-minute concert ends with a visit and dance from the Pink Panther (costume and music). The audience is large; the concert is short; everyone has a happy time. This is pure fun for students. Teachers have to be organized and plan ahead with the 5th graders. All string teachers have to be there to help. This is also a good opportunity for parent involvement. Parents are important. School administrators are always present at this concert on Saturday morning.

4. **Hamburger/hot dog cookout at the park.** Always a winner. Parents are the chefs; students are assigned to bring all other items. Teacher comes ready to play games. Maximum 3 hours. Favorite games: Circle Tag, Let's Play Zoo, and Duck, Duck, Goose. We also have volleyball and a scavenger hunt. Usually 98 percent attendance at this event. Students love the group games. Renting a covered pavilion is worth the money.

5. **May Awards Banquet. Senior Superlatives, various awards.** We try to keep price at $10.00 per person (subsidize with fundraising). Juniors are in charge of this event. 80 percent attendance. Last year 135 persons attended our banquet at a local golf club. Students enjoy dressing up.

6. **Movie Nights.** Once a semester, orchestra officers organize a movie night in our auditorium on the big screen and rent an administration-approved movie. There is no admission fee; refreshments are available. This is only for orchestra students as a chance to become better acquainted. In large orchestra programs, getting to know one another is very difficult. This is also another chance for parent involvement.

7. **Buddy Days.** At the first of school, each freshman is given an upperclassman buddy. Each nine weeks, we have a buddy day before school, 7:45 a.m. in the orchestra room, for a spirit gift exchange or for doughnuts. This is another attempt for the freshmen to know the older students. At semester, we change each orchestra to Secret Pals within the orchestra so that all students in that particular group can "do" for each other. I try to find various ways to help students make friends in the four orchestras.

8. ***Pops* Dinner Concert.** Have Booster Club organize a catered dinner (spaghetti, barbeque, or Mexican food, for example) in the school cafeteria. Sell tickets. Invite the middle school feeder orchestras to perform after dinner on the pops concert with the high school orchestra. This event provides further insight to the high school scene for orchestra and is another chance for parents to be involved and visit with middle school parents, along with the performance opportunity.

9. **Peer String Tutoring.** Organize a cluster activity with the high school students helping the 5th graders learn a string technique, i.e., bowing in lane 3. This is a two-way street of learning and socializing as well as providing teaching opportunities for the high school orchestra students.

10. **Miscellaneous get-togethers.** Dinner and playing on a river barge (on the San Antonio River) or at River Center Mall, Fiesta Texas, Sea World, and at retirement centers. Attend a ballet, an open rehearsal of the symphony, a Broadway musical with

group discounts, or a university concert (most are free). Get on mailing lists of these performing groups so that you know the event dates early in the year.

Remember that teenagers enjoy being together—whether on a short bus ride, performing a community concert, or eating breakfast tacos before school (called orchestra breakfast in Texas). The students *must* have a part in the planning of any social activity. Be sure to elect an Orchestra Council. Officers are important to the success of any activity. Give them opportunities to develop their leadership skills! Your officers will have very creative, timely ideas.

The teacher is the HAPPY FACILITATOR.

P.S. Teachers, you will learn a great deal about your students whenever you have social activities for them. The organizational time is well spent. Don't worry about the ones who did not attend. Enjoy the ones who *do* attend. Make the experience a positive one. ➥

Teaching Students to Think Musically

Beth Gilbert

"Oh! We just chopped off the end of that phrase! Did you hear it? We need to go back and fix it. You are capable of much more musicality."

INGREDIENTS:
String students, string teachers, and musical understanding.

SERVES:
Teachers looking to add more expression and musicality to their young orchestra's performance.

1. **Begin early and have high expectations.**
   Begin working on musicality the first time the students read a piece of music. It is important that they know they need to be thinking musically from the very beginning.

2. **Talk about expression.**
   Make students aware that the notes on the page are just that and they are responsible for creating the music by adding expression and feelings.

3. **Discuss the music.**
   Ask about the character of the music and what the orchestra can do to support the character. Vibrato, dynamics, bowing style, and articulation should be discussed at this time.

4. **Discuss emotions.**
   What is the emotion or feeling this section of the music brings forth? What picture is the music painting in your mind? Remind them there are no wrong answers here.

5. **Work on phrasing.**
   Allow individual students to play a phrase the way they think it should sound. Have the kids compare and contrast the different versions. How are they the same and how are they different? They need to make a choice as to which one they prefer. Ask them why they prefer one over another. Always discuss why and then they will remember it later on.

6. **Sing and play.**
   Sing a phrase together (always conduct how you want them to sing or play the phrase). Now have them play the phrase the way they sang it. Young musicians often sing with more natural phrasing and expression than they play their instruments initially.

7. **Involve everyone, not just the ones playing the melody.**
   Once the melody is played musically, ask the harmony players what they can do with

their part to support the melody in a musical way. They must learn that playing musically applies to everyone in the orchestra at all times.

8. **Record the music.**

   Students hear numerous things when listening to the recording that they miss when they are engaged in playing. Ask if they are satisfied with the phrasing and expression of the recording. Can it be better? How?

9. **Now they're ready to perform.**

   Remind them to play from the heart and not to be afraid of expressing themselves through the music. ➞●

Getting that Bow Parallel!

Robert Gillespie

INGREDIENTS:
Beginning string students, PVC tubes, rubber bands, string teacher

SERVES:
Beginning string students and string teachers of beginning students.

1. Check for readiness.

   Students should understand and be able to demonstrate an acceptable bow hand shape.

2. Model bow strokes that travel parallel to the string.

   Bow in the middle of the bow on the open D string and then on the open A string. The sounding point or contact point should be approximately halfway between the bridge and the fingerboard. Model a slow bow stroke, approximately 8 inches in length.

3. Attach a PVC tube, on top of your strings, parallel to the bridge and end of the fingerboard.

   The tube should be just wide enough for the bow to easily glide through and should be about 5 inches long. Attach the tube by placing a rubber band underneath the strings and then looping the ends of the rubber band around the ends of the tube. PVC tubing is piping that can be purchased inexpensively at hardware stores and is used for plumbing.

4. Bow through the tube with your bow traveling at a right angle to the string. The bow hair should rest flat in the tube, not angled toward the bridge or the scroll.

5. Distribute tubes and rubber bands to your students. Have them attach the tubes to their instruments.

6. Instruct students to bow through their tubes, with a good bow hand shape, at the middle of the bow with a slow bow stroke, e.g., two clicks per stroke with the metronome on 60.

7. Once students have mastered bowing through the tubes on an open string, they may begin fingering with their left hands while they are tube bowing. This helps students coordinate their parallel bowing motion while they are fingering.

Bowing at a right angle to the string is an important skill for beginning students to learn. Once mastered, students have learned the foundation for beautiful playing for the rest of their lives. For additional information, see the text *Strategies for Teaching Strings* by Donald Hamann and Robert Gillespie, Oxford University Press. Happy tube bowing! ➤●

A Succinct—but Not Necessarily Simple—Recipe for Music Making

Midori Goto

INGREDIENTS:
Health
Honesty
Dignity

SERVES:
Everyone.

There is usually something for my students to eat in my studio at USC but this recipe refers to nourishment of another kind.

1. **Attend to your health, both physical and emotional.**
    You cannot play an instrument if you are ill or in pain. Whether you have muscle or tendon ailments, back, neck, or shoulder pain, or unresolved emotional issues in your life, get the best professional help you can—as soon as possible. Your mind and body must be free of restraints in order to aspire and to create.

2. **Strive for honesty in every aspect of your life.**
    Be honest with yourself and with others. There is no partial honesty; one cannot practice honesty part-time. Acknowledge your strengths and your weaknesses, your faults and your achievements, your knowledge and ignorance. If you haven't practiced, admit this to yourself (and to your teacher), rather than pretend. Then take the necessary and realistic steps to mend the problem. Ask yourself important questions like, "Why do I want to be a musician?" or "What chance do I have to become a soloist/chamber musician/orchestral player?" Evaluate and answer them honestly. In music, being honest with yourself and those around you translates into sincerity in your playing. Be honest towards your reactions to the music, and communicate it as truthfully, honestly, and passionately to others as you can through your music. That is an important element of a personal interpretation. There is no art where there is no honesty.

3. **Behave with dignity.**
    Prepare yourself and work hard toward your musical goals. Whether you have a lesson, an audition, or a concert coming up, if you have prepared yourself mentally and physically, you can look at yourself in the mirror and know that you have done your best to prepare and that you have the potential to play your best. With dignity comes self-esteem and self-acceptance.

Each of these ingredients is essential.

Blended together, they are a potent mix.

Not only your playing, but also your life and your relationships, will be nourished. ━●

Music History in the Orchestra Rehearsal: "No-Bore Cookies"

Karin Hendricks

This recipe will turn a potentially bland serving of music history into one that your students will crave!

INGREDIENTS:
Period costumes
M&Ms
Video camera
One-page blurbs
Historical trivia
Timeline contests
Composer of the Week
Birthday parties
A dash of lecture

SERVES:
Orchestra students of any age.

1. Check for prior knowledge by quizzing students (both formally and informally) on historical eras, dates, composers, and background information about the pieces they are rehearsing.
2. Mix rehearsals alternately with above ingredients, as follows:
   - Dress up in period costume or as a particular composer and have the students perform "your" music. Coach them on particular stylistic characteristics. Tip: Many students prefer a guest composer with a snobby or arrogant attitude.
   - While teaching about the Middle Ages or Renaissance, hand out M&Ms as a mnemonic for monks and minstrels, and/or masses and motets. Since students remember better if the testing and learning environments are similar, hand out M&Ms again on test day. Similar mnemonics can of course be devised for each historical era.
   - Ask students to make a video about a particular music history era. No lecture is required—they can simply use history textbooks as a reference. This activity could take anywhere from one day to two weeks, depending on the desired depth of instruction.

     High-altitude adjustment for teachers without a video camera: Ask the students to perform in-class plays or newscasts about particular historical eras.

- When teaching a particularly demanding piece where rehearsal time is precious, hand out a one-page historical blurb about the piece that students may read during a down-time in rehearsal. While one section rehearses a tricky passage, the other students can be encouraged to pull out their blurb and read about the piece. Tip: The history pages are most meaningful to students when made from scratch. The students will appreciate reading your own description of a composer or piece, custom-made for the needs of each class, much more than a photocopied page from a published history book. Mention students by name in the blurbs for extra garnish.

    High-altitude adjustment for teachers without time to make one-page blurbs: Assign students the task of making blurbs for the class to read.

- Have contests to see how fast the students can list the major eras in music history, composer dates, works by a single composer, etc. Keep track of the record time. Optional approaches include contests between students, contests between classes, or side-by-side speedwriting on the board.
- Present a Composer of the Week where students can place guesses in a jar. Each day provide two to three clues about the composer. Post a picture of the mystery composer. On Friday, announce the composer by name and draw out a guess from the jar. Winning student receives a small prize or other educational reward.

    High-altitude adjustment for teachers without a lot of time to prepare composer clues: Assign each student a composer and a week, and have the students research and present the clues.

- Present historical trivia questions without giving an answer. On the following day, ask students for the answer to your trivia question. Reward those who did the research.
- Host birthday parties for various composers. Decorate the room (or ask students to do so). Play a piece written by the birthday composer, and celebrate with birthday cake.

3. Stir the above ingredients intermittently throughout the rehearsal process.
4. When rehearsal pieces appear golden brown (i.e., almost ready for performance), take a few moments to share additional or special insights about the pieces. This can make the piece more meaningful to the students, and will most likely add last-minute flavor to the performance.
5. Use lecture sparingly and do not overcook! Music history "no-bore cookies" are best baked in small portions over a long period of time. ➟●

Early Bow Hold (Violin/Viola)

Georgia Hornbacker

INGREDIENTS:
Beginning string students ready for their first encounter with the bow
Older string students in need of remedial bow position work
Bows marked at the balance point
A patient teacher

SERVES:
Students ready to establish or improve their bow position.

Teachers seeking a simple, effective way to establish a correct bow position.

Preparation:
1. Place a music stand with the desk in a horizontal position in front of each student.
2. Place the bow on the desk of the stand (frog to the right, hair facing the student).
3. Have students extend their left hands in a "shake hands" position.
4. Pick up the bow and lay it on the left hand.
5. Move the bow right or left until the bow balances on the hand.
6. With a pencil, make a vertical line on the stick at the balance point.

Assembly:
1. Holding the right arm at bowing height, make a circle with the thumb and long finger. Be sure the thumb points to the ceiling and the thumb and finger are vertically opposing each other on their tips.
2. Support the bow with the left hand and hold it at bowing height, placing this circle at the balance point. "Break" the circle with the stick of the bow, making sure that the thumb points to the ceiling and is as close to the student's side of the stick as possible.
3. Place all fingertips on top of the stick.
4. Push the first three fingers over the stick to the first "crease;" the line on the inside of the first joint of each finger.
5. The pinkie remains on top; tap the tip on the stick to achieve a natural curved shape.
6. Leave a small space between the index and long fingers. Long and ring fingers should touch. Also leave a small space between the ring finger and the pinkie. The base knuckles should be "squishy" and there should be a nice open oval inside the hand.
7. Allow to "set up" for one to two weeks. Then move the bow hold from the balance point to the top of the winding. After a little more "seasoning," move to the upper end of the grip or the lower end of the winding, then to the gap between the grip and the frog. Celebrate each of these "graduations" enthusiastically!

Yield:
1. Relaxed, natural bow positions.
2. Substantial reduction (if not total elimination) of scratchy sound due to tension in the bow hand and arm. This is particularly gratifying to adult beginners who are extremely sensitive to unpleasant tone.
3. Virtual elimination of the fear of dropping the bow due to the "weightless" sensation created by holding the bow at the balance point. The successive "graduations" allow the student to develop gradual control over the increased tip weight that comes with each move closer to the frog.

Substitutions: For students who are unable to hold a pencil and write their name legibly (i.e., with little fine muscle development) the Suzuki Early Bow Hold may be substituted in step 2 of assembly. Place the thumb *under* the frog directly below the gap between the grip and the frog (under the ferrule ring) and place the tip of the long finger directly above it on the stick. Continue with steps 3–6. After good control is achieved, the thumb can be moved up to the gap between the grip and the frog. This may be a longer process than that described in step 7. Each student's development will vary.

Holding the bow is a difficult skill for beginners of all ages, but this approach helps students overcome their anxieties and eases the learning process by beginning with short bows in the central portion of the bow and as their control increases using more of the bow and introducing the more sophisticated wrist and elbow movements necessary to keep the bow straight. It allows each student to progress at his/her own pace and promotes good tone quality at each step of the process. Once you have assembled this recipe with your students you can use the "condensed" version as a reminder:

"Make a circle; break the circle; tips on top; 1-2-3; tap, tap, tap."

This is an easy-to-remember prompt they can repeat each time they pick up the bow. I have used this recipe successfully with beginners, adults, and college students, and it has made my teaching and their learning more enjoyable and less stressful. Try this recipe in your studio and enjoy! ➤

Bass Pizzicato with Pizzazz

Kathleen A. Horvath

INGREDIENTS:
Any bassist who has played at least a year and desires to produce a full, rich, timely, consonant pizzicato sound

SERVES:
All bassists looking to improve their pizzicato skill and can be done while the other students in the string class are working on other skills.

1. **Establish a good open string right hand/arm pizzicato motion.**

   Have each student review the contact point of the right thumb on the fingerboard to support pizzicato. They need to identify the thumb rest spot (just above the end of the fingerboard) and mark it with a dot if necessary.

   Once the contact point has been established each student should play a whole note "circle pizzicato" on each string (Rolland "Flying Pizzicato" motion), where the attack is made and then the arm makes a circle in the air. Have each student be sure to "pull" the string with the "force" of the whole arm, not just the finger(s).

2. **Establish a good pizzicato sound on open string.**

   Have each student play an open string cycle (EEEE, AAAA, DDDD, GGGG, GGGG, DDDD, AAAA, EEEE) at a slow tempo (around quarter = 60–70) concentrating on making good contact with the string and getting an "on-time" attack as well as a rich full sound. Remind the student to use the whole arm rather than just the hand so that the fingers do not tire so easily. Once the basic motion is developed, basses can echo any open string patterns using this good pizzicato motion and attack.

3. **Developing a supportive left hand through "pulling" sound.**

   Have each student begin by tapping all four fingertips on the D string with a steady quarter-note pulse of 60. Keeping the pulse with the left hand is a challenge, but with careful practice it will become easy. Now that the student is able to play an accurate pulse with the left hand, have him depress the string into the fingerboard by "pulling" the string from the left arm and shoulder. Each quarter note should be pulled into the string by the fingers while being supported by the thumb and then released just before the next quarter note. Perform this a few times and repeat as necessary to unlock the shoulder, arm, and hand. This may take a few sessions if the instrument balance depends on the thumb for most of the support. No clamping with the left thumb and fingers. Expand this exercise to all four strings.

After the "pulling" motion is comfortable, have each student "pull" the string into the fingerboard so quickly that the pitch F♯ is produced.

Once a pitch is produced with the left hand only, then the student is ready to combine both hands.

The core of a good pizzicato sound on a closed pitch comes from the left hand. While it is true that the right hand produces the pitch, the left hand establishes the contact of the string with the fingerboard. So, for a student to get a good pizzicato sound the string has to be fully depressed onto the fingerboard.

Many bassists do not depress the string fully to the fingerboard and that can result in a "thunk" pizzicato rather than an actual pitch. This can be remedied by "pulling" the string into the fingerboard rather than "squeezing." This should also relieve the pressure on the thumb to be responsible for "squeezing" and the fingers will be more flexible since they are not exerting force against the thumb.

Also, be careful that the arm is not excessively low with a pronounced bend in the wrist. Students who lack strength in the upper torso will have trouble supporting the left arm, and the elbow will end up drooping very low, creating an excessive bend in the wrist. This both robs the player of depressive force to pull the string and makes it hard to maintain a good left hand shape so intonation also suffers.

In general, in the positions up to the octave, the elbow is always slightly lower than the wrist, maintaining a relatively straight line between the middle finger and elbow. A bassist playing in the first position will have a relatively high arm (the upper arm will almost be parallel to the floor). Because this location of the fingerboard is largely where many young players spend a great deal of time in orchestra situations, it is critical that they develop the adequate muscle strength. When the student tires, it is time to stop and wait until the next session.

4. **Establish a good pizzicato sound on a closed pitch.**
   After each student has an on time, rhythmically accurate, consonant pizzicato sound on an open string and has developed the "pulling" motion for the supportive left hand, it is now time to put it all together. Have each student pick a familiar, easy melody such as "Hot Cross Buns" and play it slowly (quarter note = 60) using pizzicato. Have each student pay careful attention to resetting the right hand after playing each note and simultaneously pulling the string with the left hand so that the note sounds clearly. Once the student is able to perform this simple melody with an on time, consonant pitch, it is time to speed up the tempo and try this technique with other favorite melodies.

   Repeat this process daily (about 5 minutes) so that both right and left hand strength grow for pizzicato with pizzazz.

5. **"Boogie" Bass.**
   Pick any piece that utilizes a "walking" or tonic/dominant march bass line and let the basses show you how it is done. The pitches will ring because the left hand is pulling into the string while the right hand executes the pizzicato. Walking a "line" is an essential skill for all bassists, and careful review of these exercises will keep the hands in perfect pizzicato shape.

Teaching Cello and Bass Vibrato

James Kjelland

Most students are fascinated with vibrato from the very start. Some will try on their own despite instructions to the contrary, some will "pester" you to teach it to them, others will feel they are not ready. I believe strongly that the foundation of vibrato can be established within the first year of instruction by way of motion/action games in the tradition of Paul Rolland methodology. The sooner you start, the better, for a number of reasons. The following is a series of actions that lead to a smooth, relaxed motion that translates into a beautiful sound. Just as with any skill, the learning rate from step to step will vary greatly between students but it is important to master each step before moving ahead. The following tips refer to both instruments unless otherwise indicated.

INGREDIENTS:
Students of any age who are ready to learn vibrato
Instruments in good working order
Understanding of basic instrument and hand position

SERVES:
Teachers and students of cello or bass vibrato.

1. **Readiness?**
   Because of the sequential nature of this program, step 1 can begin virtually at any time once basic instrument and hand position are stabilized. The process is a matter of developing correct motions that progress to the ultimate goal—a beautiful sound. Early vibrato motions, while still far from mastery, also go a long way toward improving overall coordination and relaxation, especially in the left hand.

2. **What's it about?**
   Motivate through sound as well as image. Demonstrate for your students with and without vibrato and play video and audio recordings of different styles from famous artists including different style periods. Encourage students to visualize themselves moving and sounding the same, i.e., program their visual learning.

3. **Start cooking.**
   Basically this progression of vibrato skills goes from larger to smaller and slower to faster. Teaching of vibrato can take place simultaneously with, but separate from, the agenda of music reading, intonation, basic bowings, etc.

a. Begin by locating the left hand in approximately fourth position with the thumb at or close to the base of the neck and *not pressing*. To guarantee this, take the thumb off the neck entirely to remove the temptation but keep it under the second finger as in normal playing. Then, placing the second finger (only) on the fingerboard between two strings, glide up and down with a light touch. This should be a motion from the elbow joint, not the wrist or shoulder, i.e., the upper arm is the power source. (Use a tissue under the fingertip to reduce friction if necessary.) The distance the fingertip travels on the fingerboard should be about 8 inches and the motion should be rhythmically steady—about one cycle (up and down) per quarter note at moderato 4/4 tempo. At the end of each downward motion (toward the bridge) the thumb should bump against the base of the neck. This will help keep the tempo steady.

b. Still with a light touch, move the fingertip to the D string without the thumb pressing and without the string pressed to the fingerboard. Gradually increase the speed to about eight to ten eighth-note cycles per bow while narrowing the width of the motion to about 2–3 inches. A metronome may be helpful at this point.

c. Now introduce the bow. Draw a smooth whole bow (or at least half) while maintaining the left hand gliding motion—about eight to twelve cycles. Basses will be on the slower side of these recommended speeds! This exercise is at the core of vibrato coordination and may take time to master. The sound will be a whistling tone because it is all harmonics. Be sure to maintain a light touch on the string while the bow applies weight equivalent to a forte dynamic level, i.e., the bow is "heavier" on the string than the left hand. Muscles in the left arm will get tired! But there should be no discomfort.

d. Once these actions are coordinated (which may take a while), gradually increase the speed to about sixteenth-note cycles while narrowing the motion to less than an inch. Shoot for sixteen cycles per bow. Take whatever amount of time is needed to get this smooth, even, and relaxed. If tension sets in, back up to a point where the tension is gone and gradually increase again.

e. When this becomes easy, gradually transfer more arm weight to the fingertip while the motion continues at a steady speed. When the string touches the fingerboard, the fingertip will no longer be gliding up and down, but the arm will continue in exactly the same motion! The result will be a solid tone on a steady pitch (approximately A or B♭).

f. Now you're ready to do the same process with the other fingers in the recommended sequence: 3, 1, 4 for cello and 1, 4 for bass. Care should always be taken to maintain the arm motion smoothly and rhythmically while the bow is drawn at a steady speed.

g. From this point, repeat the process (from item b. above) in first position—slower and wider to faster and narrower. In this location the arm is no longer opening and closing at the elbow but swinging in a relaxed balanced way. Another way to create this sensation is to place the arm in playing position (elbow out to the side, without the instrument) with the second finger touching the collarbone. Let the forearm "rock and roll" in a continuous cyclic motion. This motion assures that no twisting of the forearm or flexing at the wrist is happening. The muscles of the upper arm should feel loose and floppy.

h. (The following item can be added after "e." above if you prefer.) Now it is time to slightly increase the speed of the vibrato to the point that it transforms into a beautiful tone—just a bit faster than the moderato sixteenths. Be very careful that the motion does not degenerate into a spasm or quiver. If this happens, back up to a tempo that is relaxed and work up to it until the spasm is gone. Check to make sure you are not squeezing the thumb!

4. **Cool and serve.** Once a smooth vibrato is achieved in the above exercises, find occasional notes in the music that are sustained enough to practice this new vibrato skill. Start with the "easy" fingers (two or three) and expand from there. Slower movements are of course more conducive to this but sustained notes in any context can be used for vibrato practice.

Great vibrato is the result of patient and persistent practice. The gliding motions described above are key to developing fundamental coordination as well as correcting problems that may surface along the way. It is also key to developing the smooth transfer of vibrato from one finger to another in melodic playing. If you develop a "hitch" in the motion, go back the gliding (with bow) until the coordination is re-established. Please avoid twisting the forearm, i.e., "turning a door knob," to get the pitch oscillation! This is exactly the wrong motion, although, to the untrained observer, it appears that that is what is happening. Such twisting will interfere with control of speed, width, and intonation. Finally, speed and width can vary according to dynamic intensity, pitch range, and string length. This progressive gliding approach facilitates the development and control of these variables as well. ➤●

Getting into Good Playing Position

Dottie Ladman

INGREDIENTS:
Beginning string students at their first lesson, properly sized instruments, shoulder rests (or sponges)

SERVES:
Violin and viola students and their teachers.

1. **Learn "rest position."**
   Students hold instruments under the right arm with the bridge facing away from their body, right elbow hugging the chin rest, and scroll tilted slightly up so it is in front of the chest.

2. **Learn to bow.**
   Face forward, feet together, bend at the waist and show the audience the top of your head while silently saying "hippopotamus."

3. **Shoulders.**
   When the teacher says "shoulders," the students turn to their right so their left shoulders are toward the teacher, put their feet a shoulder width apart, and put their left hands on the bottom shoulder of the instrument (the one closest to the floor), sliding the hand up to the neck so it is touching the neck where it meets the body of the instrument.

4. **One.**
   When the teacher says "one," the students lift their instruments up with their left hand so they are standing like the Statue of Liberty. Scrolls are pointed at the ceiling.

5. **Two.**
   When the teacher says "two," the students turn their instruments upside down by rotating their left hand (the one holding the instrument) counterclockwise. Now the scrolls are pointed at the floor.

6. **Three.**
   When the teacher says "three," the students place the instrument on the left shoulder, covering the shoulder. The scrolls are now pointing at the teacher. Students then turn their heads and place the jaw in the chin rest, with the chin near the tailpiece, and adjust for comfort.

7. **Hug.**

When the students have the proper placement they lower their left hands and "hug" the instrument with their shoulder and jaw. If the instrument is properly sized and placed and the shoulder rest is appropriate, this is a very easy thing for them to do, and they instantly have great position! Try to hold the "hug" for a count of ten.

8. **"L-icopter."**

Have students return their left hands to the shoulder of their instruments. With the right hand, form a backwards "L" with the thumb and first finger. This is the "L-icopter." They fly the L-icopter around and around, and finally land it on its "landing pad," which is the right corner of the fingerboard as they are looking at it.

9. **Pluck.**

With the pointer finger of the L-icopter, students pluck the strings. Put a chart of the violin and viola bridges, showing the names of the strings on the wall, and have the students play each of the strings by name.

10. **Play a song.**

What is a first lesson without playing some music? Show students how to play the 12-bar blues in D (16 D's, 8 G's, 8 D's, 4 A's, 4 G's, 8 D's), or "Ants:"

Eek, eek, eek, all the little

Ants, ants, ants, digging in the

Dirt, dirt, dirt, digging under

Ground, ground, ground, all the way to

China, China, China

11. **Reinforce.**

Have students go through the Getting into Position sequence every time before playing, repeating whenever playing position deteriorates, until it becomes second nature and the students don't even have to think about it any more. Encourage, praise, reward, and enjoy having students who look great when they play. ➞

A Great Recording of Your Orchestra, Chamber Ensemble or Student

Scott D. Laird

Whether desired for archival purposes, audition recordings, rehearsal enrichment, or for some other purpose, string teachers have struggled for years with the theory, technology, and process of making good quality recordings. Hopefully, this recipe will aid in the creation of many great recordings by string educators! It is really not that difficult.

INGREDIENTS:
A well-prepared ensemble or soloist
Some carefully chosen equipment
Musically experienced ears
Willingness to learn through some trial and error

SERVES:
Teachers and students wanting to make high-quality recordings of their performances.

1. Prepare your musicians for the date of recording by carefully rehearsing the music to be recorded. Remember: recordings do not lie!
2. Secure the following equipment for the recording:
   a. 2 matching microphones—preferably condenser microphones (or 1 stereo condenser microphone). These are the input transducer and are extremely important to the outcome of the recording. Condenser microphones range in price from around $100 to well over $1,000. Good-sounding condenser microphones can be found in the lower end of that range. The AKG C1000 S is a good choice for around $200, and the Audio Technica AT 2020 is a fine choice for around $100.
   b. 2 microphone stands—taller is always better.
   c. Proper microphone cables—most schools have these around the auditorium facility, or they can be purchased for about $20 each.
   d. A digital recording device with a CD burner—most teachers now have a computer that will serve this function. Any desktop or laptop computer with a CD burner and a USB interface will serve as a high-quality digital recorder.
   e. An audio interface with USB connections for your computer—there are many on the market today. It must have two microphone inputs to allow for a stereo recording and have "phantom power" to ensure proper operation of your condenser microphones (condenser microphones require power, and phantom

power simply sends an electrical charge from the interface to the microphone, essentially "turning it on.") The Lexicon Lambda sells for around $200 and is an excellent choice. There are many others on the market. Most come with free recording software as well.

  f. Appropriate recording and editing software. If your audio interface does not come with software, download a free copy of Audacity from the Web. It is open-source software (free and available to all) and works great!

3. Practice setting up and running the equipment before the day of the recording. Preparation is always desirable! Find a student or parent from your ensemble that is interested and ask them to help. There is one in every crowd!

4. Choose the room for the recording. Typically large ensembles use large rooms and smaller ensembles or soloists use smaller rooms. Avoid rooms with odd acoustics such as slaps or fast echoes. A nice reverb, however, is desirable. Avoid rooms with concrete walls or all parallel walls. Often, the school auditorium or a local church is the best choice for any size of ensemble.

5. Properly place the microphones in the room. In order to do this, you must use your hearing and a bit of trial and error. The goal is to create a good stereo recording. That is—each microphone corresponds to a human's ears. One will pick up the sounds that the left ear hears and one will pick up the sounds that the right ear hears. A great starting point is to simply walk through the room while the ensemble is playing and choose the spot where you find the sound to be the most pleasing. Chances are, the microphones will, too. Typically, microphones will be closer for a soloist (as close as 6–8 feet) and farther away for a large ensemble (as far as 20 feet or more).

6. The two most common microphone configurations for a live recording are a "coincident pair" and a "spaced pair." Try both before deciding on one. A coincident pair employs two microphones placed with the grills touching, angled apart, at a height above the ensemble. The left microphone picks up the right side of the orchestra (representing the hearing in your right ear) and the right microphone picks up the left side of the orchestra (representing the hearing in your left ear). The result is a recording that allows the listener to perceive the location of all of the instruments. Begin with the microphones at a 90-degree angle. A wider angle causes the listener to perceive a wider spacing of the ensemble. A spaced pair employs two microphones placed 4-6 feet apart, aimed directly at the ensemble, at a height above the ensemble. More width between the microphones causes the listener to perceive a wider spacing of the ensemble.

7. When you are happy with the microphone placement, begin the recording session. Have the orchestra play the loudest section of music that you will be recording and be sure that the equipment is not "clipping" or "distorting." This is usually represented by a red light on the audio interface. Adjust the "gain" or "microphone level" on the interface to ensure a distortion-free recording. Try recording each piece once, and then going back to rerecord those that you are not happy with. This tends to make the session less tedious for the musicians. Record each piece until you are happy with the performance.

8. After the session is over, use the software to trim the excess space from the beginning and end of each track and to "normalize" each piece. These are basic functions of recording software and can be easily mastered with very little time or experience. Normalizing is the process of raising the overall level of a track to its maximum without distorting. Be sure to save the original copies of the recording.

9. Using your CD burner's software, put the tracks in order and burn a CD. ➤

Project Ideas to Supplement Concert Music

Lori Lauff

When learning concert music, consider supplementing with interesting projects like compositions, reflections, and coloring. Extra experiences like these will often stay with students for a lifetime.

INGREDIENTS:
Students with an interest in exploring their creativity, teachers interested in providing a framework for creativity, music, pencil, paper, and crayons (computers are optional).

SERVES:
All participating students for a lifetime.

A Composition Recipe*
1. Choose an appropriate-level piece to perform at an upcoming concert.
2. Using a bass line (or ostinato) found somewhere in the music, select an eight-measure section that can be used as the duet part. (Once students are comfortable with eight measures, feel free to try longer compositions.)
3. Ask students to compose an original melody that can be played on top of the bass line part.
4. Have students perform their original melody for the class with some classmates playing the bass line. Recording compositions is always fun, too!

*If a computer lab is available, install the free program Finale Notepad (www.codamusic.com). Ask students to set up the page in a duet format so they can type in the assigned bass line notes. Then, as they compose their melodies, students can hear what the pieces will sound like and will be able to make changes as desired. Always remind students that they need to be able to play what they compose. This assignment could also be done using regular staff paper and a pencil.

A Reflection Recipe*
Invite students to write a reaction paper based on their favorite or least favorite piece played during the school year (or each quarter/semester).

1. Give a specific mission. For example, ask them to use the sheet music as a reference and select one piece that has been a favorite or least favorite.
2. Specify the requirements of each paragraph. For example, in the first paragraph, give a detailed description of the piece using only the facts and describe what happens musically in the piece using correct music terms. In the second paragraph, share your opinions about why you selected the piece and explain why it was your favorite or least favorite. In the third paragraph, explain why you would recommend or not rec-

ommend that future orchestras should play the piece. Remember to always support opinions with specific examples from the music.

3. Make expectations clear using a grading rubric. Ideas for categories would be:
   a. Ideas & Content (detailed description of piece with musical terms used, insight into why piece was selected, clarity of own reaction to the piece, clarity of recommendation for future use, opinions supported with evidence from music)
   b. Voice (feelings/opinions are expressed fully, shows personal connection, vivid and descriptive style)
   c. Word Choice (musical vocabulary is used correctly)
   d. Organization (beginning, middle, end, and paragraphs are well organized)
   e. Conventions (spelling, grammar, punctuation)
   f. Presentation (heading, title, paragraphs, final copy form—typed or blue/black ink)

Again, if computer space is available, students could type these reaction papers. This more easily allows students to edit. Many students also like to personalize their papers with creative fonts, colors, and clip art. However, handwriting works perfectly fine for this assignment as well.

A Coloring Recipe

When selecting concert music, try to make one connection with a piece of artwork. For example, Smetana was inspired by his homeland to compose *Ma Vlast,* which includes *The Moldau* (good student arrangements available). Smetana painted a beautiful picture of the Bohemian landscape and river through his music. Georgia O'Keefe created *Blue and Green Music* (1919), an abstract landscape painting, which was inspired by the forested lands surrounding Lake George, New York. Using a connection such as this, create an easy abstract coloring assignment.

1. Show students an example of the artwork. Consider copying it for the students, or put it in a sleeve to safely pass it around the class. The Art Institute of Chicago is a great resource (www.artic.edu).
2. Provide a short explanation for the students, making any connections between the artist and the composer. Biographical information for both the artist and composer is a good place to start.
3. Then, listen to a recording of the piece. As students listen, have them create their own abstract artwork that corresponds to the piece of music being played.
4. Consider placing the artwork in a binder to present at an upcoming concert. Take a minute to explain the project to parents at the concert. ➤●

Recipe for a Healthy Viola Sound

Dee Martz

INGREDIENTS:
1 violist with well-aligned body posture
1 properly adjusted viola with four fresh strings
1 shoulder pad or sponge—must be fit to each unique combination of viola and violist
1 viola bow with good hair, adequately rosined
1 bow hand—relaxed and balanced

SERVES:
Violists seeking more resonance in their sound.

Take a violist with well-aligned posture. Add a viola by placing it on the left shoulder. Lift the bow with a balanced, supple right hand. Put the bow on the C string and sink the hair into the string using arm weight. Pull the bow from the frog to the tip across the open C string using a long, circular bow motion. Repeat as necessary on all the open strings. Experienced cooks may also push the bow in tip-to-frog circles. The bow hand should feel the friction as the bow moves the string. Imitate the open string sound on other notes. When it is well done, the jawbone and scroll will vibrate freely due to the rich overtones and sympathetic vibrations.

For best results:
Recheck posture often, as it can go bad without warning.
Use rosin sparingly.
Discard all bow holds and bow grips.
Avoid digging and pressing.
Remember that intonation influences tone. ●➔

Teaching Violin/Viola Vibrato

Joanne May

"Just wiggle your finger! No, not like that . . . take your wrist and move it back and forth . . . but you still have to hear the pitch change . . . um . . . try taking off your thumb . . . careful! Watch out–your violin is slipping . . . hold on! No, don't hold so tightly!"

INGREDIENTS:
Enthusiastic string students who are ready to learn vibrato and string teachers.

SERVES:
Violin and viola students, their teachers, and those who hear them perform.

1. **Check for readiness.**
    Students should be able to play consistently in tune and be able to finger independently.

2. **Model a good vibrato.**
    Demonstrate for your students a melody without, then with, vibrato. Discuss the quality and expression it adds to the tone.

3. **Listen to recordings of various types of vibrato.**
    Listen to both instrumental and vocal vibratos. Early music ensembles are excellent examples of minimal or no vibrato. Contrast this with slow music from the romantic era.

4. **Do pre-vibrato exercises.**
    Train students in the movement of vibrato with waving, tapping, and brushing exercises with and without the instrument. Use a tissue on the fingerboard to help students' fingers to slide back and forth. "Knuckle-knocking" (knock the left index knuckle against the pegs), "finger wiggles" (make a circle with left thumb and a finger, wiggle the joints of the finger to aid flexibility), and "bump-finger" (point right index finger at left vibrating finger, let it bump to feel the evenness of the movement) can be effective in encouraging good vibrato movement.

5. **Now they're ready.**
    Work without the bow. Begin in guitar position, then brush the whole hand up and down the fingerboard with fingertips rounded on top of the strings. Make the movement smaller, stick the thumb, then stick the second or third finger. While still wiggling, move the instrument into shotgun position, then move the instrument to the left shoulder, then tip the instrument into playing position. Shake out tension. Repeat.

Once students have mastered the movement, have them secure their instruments by leaning against a wall with the scroll. Have them work in pairs—one does vibrato leaning against a wall while the other bows across the string. Repeat over and over. Switch partners. Have successful students demonstrate for the class with their partners. When students are comfortable doing the movement, have them try playing vibrato with their own bows.

6. **Video performances.**

    Get a 10-second close up video of the students' hands. Play the video for the class and have everyone evaluate the movement and sound. If you can record only the hands and not the faces of the students, the class can guess who they're watching.

7. **Use a CBR (Calculator Based Ranger).**

    Your math or science department may have this device. It is a sonic motion detector that graphs the vibrato movement onto a graphing calculator. Once you take the students' samples, you can determine the speed and amplitude of each student's vibrato and show the resulting graphs.

8. **Work with a metronome.**

    Play two, three, four, five, and six wiggles per second. This practice aids the student in control of the vibrato motion.

9. **Incorporate vibrato into music.**

    Find occasional notes in music that are good choices for vibrato. The students' first attempt may be only a final note of a piece. Second- and third-fingered notes are the best choices. At first be sure the notes are long enough for the student to have time to get their vibrato moving.

Violin and viola vibrato is a very unnatural movement. When you break up the process of learning vibrato into small steps, encourage repetition, and help students avoid bad habits from forming, they will become very capable of performing this skill in a fairly short period of time. Continue to encourage your students, help them refine the movement, and celebrate their successes! ➤●

Incorporating Vibrato into the Warm-up Routine

Peter Miller

"My students' limited ability to produce expressive vibrato (they sound like a flock of nanny-goats) seems to persist despite the fact that I encourage them to work on it and we do address it when we can . . . I have a warm-up routine that includes scales, arpeggios, rhythmic, and technical exercises . . . how can I integrate vibrato development efficiently into the routine?"

INGREDIENTS:
String students in their seats doing the warm-up routine perhaps while the *teacher* is recording attendance

SERVES:
Middle and high school string orchestra members.

1. Set up a routine for various warm-ups and introduce vibrato component when students are able to easily shift to the first partial (mid-string) harmonic. Have students sound the harmonic on the G string touching gently with the tip of the soft pad of the fourth finger (including cellists and bassists for this exercise). Once this is established, have students gently slide their fingers from the harmonic pitch to a half step below it with the following rhythm (fig. a):

Fig. a.

Violinists and violists should let their wrists rest against the rib of the instrument, with the motion from the wrist. Cellists and bassists utilize an "up and down" vertical motion of the forearm with a stable wrist. When first learning the rhythm, use separate bows then slur half the pattern in one stroke, finally all in one bow. Once this is accomplished, have all students then play the pattern on the same harmonic G pitch using the third finger, then second and first. This includes bassists (why not prepare for playing with the third finger in the *"lower* stratosphere" of thumb position?). Students should be encouraged to keep their fingers relaxed and almost straight, with a minimum of curvature.

2. Once students can perform the above rhythm in one bow with fourth, third, second, first fingers, then have them play the designated down bow pattern followed by an up bow with a free, gentle, and relaxed harmonic "ghost" vibrato (fig b). Point out to them that with the exercises they are learning, they will, with regular patient and careful practice, be able to accomplish "regular" vibrato with the same ease. This should be a foretaste of what vibrato will feel like.

Fig. b.

3. Establish third position by having the students to play C on the G string with the first finger. Then have all students (including cellists and bassists) play D with the second finger, E with the third, and F with the fourth. Students then play the harmonic G with the pinkie (it is an extension for the violinists and violists). This establishes a major pattern, which will assist in creating a pattern as the exercise is completed. These fingerings of course are customary for violinists and violists, not for cellists and bassists. You can reassure them that the entire ensemble is practicing uniform finger exercises, and that they are "very special" because they are adding the element of pitch matching with unconventional small shifts. Have the musicians practice this pattern ascending and descending. Once it is played accurately and easily, we may proceed to the next step and start putting our routine together.

4. Students will play just the rhythmic pattern (without the previous up bow harmonic "Ghost Vibrato") in one bow first with the fourth finger harmonic on G, then fourth finger depressing the string one step below on F. If using the pinkie alone presents a problem for a student, have him/her depress both the fourth and third fingers together with the fourth on the F pitch, the third a half step below, and proceed using both fingers simultaneously. Prior to playing, have the ensemble practice the fourth finger oscillation without the bow saying aloud "straight-back-straight-back" while the fingers perform the rhythmic pattern (fig. c, "/" designates straight, "–" designates back).

Fig. c.

The finger starts in a relatively vertical placement on the pitch then comes back to an almost horizontal plane when pulled back for the lower part of the oscillation. For most students, the finger will "snap" back and forth. Point out that this is normal and that one of the reasons we are practicing this exercise is to create muscular control and flexibility in these fingers. Students should focus on relaxed fingers, pulling each finger back almost flat against the string on the lower pitch part of the oscillation (vibrato oscillates from the pitch to below the pitch; otherwise the pitch will sound out of tune, too sharp). Use separate bows, then half pattern to bow, ultimately a single bow for the entire pattern. After the fourth finger, repeat the same procedure with the third finger on the pitch E, the second on D, and the first on C. Once this pattern is learned, do the same on the D string (the pitches are harmonic D, then CBAG), then the A string, and E and C strings. A descending pattern of E string followed by, A, D, G, and C can be easily integrated into the string ensemble warm-up routine.

5.   Once students have some facility with the rhythmic pattern, follow the down bow pattern with free vibrato up bow as we did previously on the harmonics (fig. b). Emphasize slow and relaxed motion, with the fingers pulling back flat as much as possible. It may be useful to practice the up bow vibrato in eighth, triplet, and sixteenth rhythms before introducing free vibrato. In any case, a free and relaxed motion without excessive speed and intensity is desirable.

This exercise may be used in later stages of development to strengthen expressive vibrato, integrating more muscular involvement for more speed and/or intensity as well as amount of oscillation. Integrating vibrato into the rehearsal routine lets students know that you "mean business" when it comes to vibrato, and may provide them with an easily implemented regular component in their personal practice routine. ➜

A Baguette Buffet of Alternative Styles

Steve Muise

INGREDIENTS:
All string players—yes, guitars can play too! Community members, young and old, and anyone who can carry a tune. The desire to play and learn using a variety of teaching styles.

SERVES:
Any string player with a nationality, the desire to have tunes "in your pocket," and the ability to arrange and improvise! Great for school orchestra teachers!

1. **Mixing and Rising: Discovery Phase**
   - Discuss personal identity, culture, and nationality with your students.
   - Have students describe the folk and traditional music and dance that they know.
   - Learn how composers use familiar music as a compositional technique.
   - Listen to Copeland, Bartok, etc.
   - Listen to any music that uses strings in a non-classical fashion (folk fiddlers of all kinds, modern quartets, rock, jazz, klezmer, mariachi).

2. **Baking: Preheat the Oven—Practice the Techniques**
   - Have students play easy familiar folk tunes; demonstrate and encourage kids to do their own theme and variation. Example: "Hot Cross Buns"
   - Less experienced students may just want to experiment with a sound palette; experienced students should be encouraged to vary rhythmic sequence and melodic phrasing.
   - Work with students to develop simple harmonic outline (level appropriate: perhaps with less experienced players, give them right and wrong examples to choose from to promote success . . . more experienced players can "play" their way through discovering the changes).
   - This is a great opportunity to relate key to scale and the modulating "key of the moment." How often do we ask our kids what the key signature tells us, but not relate it to the actual harmony?
   - Discover appropriate accompaniment patterns that involve all students—bass patterns, rhythmic patterns (on instrument or clapping, etc.), chords.

3. **Breaking Bread: Implementation and Enjoyment**
   - Encourage students to choose music from multiple genres and styles . . . mini idea bank: hip hop, disco, historical eras, barbershop. They'll know what they like, and they'll learn to appreciate other styles.
   - Have them develop the accompaniment harmony, and patterns.

- Guide them through an arrangement: again, level appropriate . . . perhaps younger students decide who plays melody, older students create introductions, tags, solos, etc., and more.

4. **Toast (Add Jam!): What to Do to Keep It Fresh (Add Jamming!)**
   - Invite community members who play alternative styles in to join you. Note: This doesn't necessarily have to be string players . . . perhaps there's a rock band that would want to collaborate, or a jazz saxophonist or a drum circle member . . . variety will open up your students' minds (and yours too!)
   - Many schools have extracurricular groups to highlight their large ensembles . . . show choir, musicals, jazz band, marching band . . . what do we have?
   - Start an alternative styles ensemble at your school, invite a full rhythm section, work with dancers, collaborate!
   - Attend (and then perhaps perform) at a community dance. Contradances are very popular in the Northeast. There are pockets of community dances throughout the world. Dancing will help students feel the beat and the intended "lift" that needs to be inherent in many alternative styles and forms of music.
   - Field trip to see concerts, put on concerts, play for people, and collaborate! There is much to learn from the people around you!

Your students (and you) will benefit from the social interactions, greater understanding of the fundamentals of music, and connections to the world around us. Have fun!

Planning a Successful Rehearsal

Debra K. Myers

The secret to a successful rehearsal is in the planning, which is done prior to the rehearsal. Much in the same way as a cook prepares the ingredients prior to assembling the recipe, a director must prepare for a rehearsal by studying the scores, playing the parts, and sequencing/balancing the ingredients (activities) to maximize student understanding and success.

INGREDIENTS:
20 stands of string students (more or less is fine, depending on the blend you desire)
3–4 different sets of skill-appropriate orchestra literature (NO photocopies)
3–4 scores, previously studied
Pencils (a minimum of one per student)
Several colored pencils/highlighters
1 baton
1 tuner
1 metronome

SERVES:
Teachers, students, and their audiences.

1. **PLAN:** Determine your goals for the ensemble. Choose year-long, quarterly, monthly, weekly, and daily goals. Make goals specific and realistic.

2. **SELECT:** Choose a variety of literature that will enable you to accomplish your goals. Enlist the help of colleagues when needed.

3. **STUDY:** Study the scores of the literature you have selected. Use colored pencils and/or highlighters to mark entrances, dynamics, repeats, tempo changes, bowings, etc.

4. **PLAY:** Play each instrument part through on the corresponding instrument. Decide on fingerings/positions and make any bowing corrections. Enlist the help of advanced students for their technical expertise. Use colored pencils/highlighters to mark challenging sections.

5. **PRACTICE:** Practice your conducting gestures in front of a mirror. Use a metronome to help establish correct tempos. The use of a baton is strongly encouraged. Listen to recordings where available.

6. **REHEARSE:** Write a rehearsal plan. Include the following ingredients:

- A tuning procedure
- An intonation study (left hand focus)
  This could be "copy-cat," "I play . . . you play," etc. using difficult passages from the music being studied, or a corresponding scale.
- An articulation study (right hand focus)
  This could be a difficult bowing pattern or troublesome rhythm on a corresponding scale. Utilize "skeleton bowing"—isolating the rhythm or passage on corresponding open strings.
- Repetition of difficult passages/sections. Give students strategies for practicing these sections. Remember to rehearse at different tempos. Be creative in expanding horizontally before allowing students to move forward.
- Feedback. Provide both positive and negative feedback of student work. Be specific in verbal instructions. Say, "Second violins, your F♯ on the third beat of measure 32 is very flat." Don't say, "Seconds, you play really out of tune in that section." Enlist the ears of your students in rehearsal diagnostics and remember to record rehearsals for critical listening outside of the classroom.

7. **ASSEMBLE AND ENJOY!** Reassemble the sections your students have rehearsed and practiced, remaining true to the composers' intent. As an added treat, have students listen to professional recordings of the literature they are studying, if available. Enjoy the tasteful and beautiful work you have created! ➞●

Developing Easy Scalar Improvisation

Martin Norgaard

INGREDIENTS:
String student, teacher, and an open mind. Any student can be his or her own teacher. Any teacher can continue to learn as a student.

SERVES:
All string players.

Before the development of notation, all music was partially improvised (Ferand, 1961[1]). Initially Western notation was so ambiguous that performers were still improvising around melodies loosely implied by written symbols. With the advent of more precise notation, improvisation in Western classical music slowly disappeared. Yet improvisation was considered a vital skill up through the middle of the nineteenth century and was often featured in performances by virtuosi (Goertzen, 1998[2]). In the oral folk traditions where no notation was adapted, ethnographical research shows that tunes were not transmitted from player to player exactly, but that an element of improvisation was part of nearly all performance (Nettl, 1998[3]). Improvisation is evident in Ambrosian and Gregorian Chant, baroque instrumental music, Indian music, nineteenth-century classical soloist performance, jazz, Cantonese opera, American fiddle music, and more. Great improvisers include J. S. Bach, Mozart, Clara Schumann (improvised preludes to composed pieces in concert), Charlie Parker, Buddy Guy, Mark O'Connor, and L. Subramaniam.

Here is an easy way to introduce improvisation to your students. Your students more than likely improvised vocally as they were developing their singing voices from age 1–4 (Moog, 1976[4]). The recipe below is a way of transferring what they already know (but may have forgotten) to their instruments.

1. Play a two-octave scale ascending and descending using quarter notes.
2. Play the same scale as above but add a rhythm given by the teacher to each note. The rhythm and articulation of the notes should be in the style and meter of the improvisation to be developed (e.g., for classical baroque style use separated notes; for jazz use swing rhythms etc.). Here is an example in baroque style:

Continue

3. Play the same scale as above but change pitch on each note. For the rhythm above it would look like this:

Continue

4. Repeat steps 2 and 3 but use rhythms suggested by the student.
5. Ask the student to play the scale but change rhythms randomly throughout the two octaves. It could look like this:

Continue

6. Explain that the student is currently changing direction on the top root. In other words, the top note in a two octave G-major scale is the note G, and that is where "we currently change direction and go back down the scale."
7. Invite the student to play the scale with improvised rhythms, as in step 5, but change direction on a different note than the top root.
8. Ask the student to choose a new bottom note other than the lower root and suggest that coming down the scale, "we could change direction on this note and go back up the scale."
9. Invite the student to play up and down the scale with varied rhythms changing direction on various notes. It could look like this.

Continue

10. Explain the difference between steps and skips and point out that the student is currently improvising with steps only.
11. Invite the student to incorporate skips. Smaller skips, such as a third, are easier to use. The final improvisation could look something like this.

Continue

1 Ferand, E. (1961). Improvisation in nine centuries of western music: An anthology with a historical introduction. In K. G. Fellerer (Ed.), *Anthology of music*. Koln: Arno Volk Verlag.

2 Goertzen, V. W. (1998). Setting the stage: Clara Schumann's preludes. In B. Nettl & M. Russell (Eds.), *In the course of performance: Studies in the world of musical improvisation* (pp. 237–260). Chicago: University of Chicago Press.

3 Nettl, B. (1998). An art neglected in scholarship. In B. Nettl & M. Russell (Eds.), *In the course of performance: Studies in the world of musical improvisation* (pp. 1–26). Chicago: University of Chicago Press.

4 Moog, H. (1976). *The musical experience of the pre-school child* (C. Clarke, Trans.). London: Schott.

Teaching Independent Listening for Successful Ensemble Performance

Ray Ostwald

For confident vertical alignment in orchestra and chamber music performances!

INGREDIENTS:
An orchestra of string students who have learned a piece or pieces "pretty well"
A director

SERVES:
Orchestra students and their teachers.

Pre-preparation:
    a. Have students regularly take turns sitting in the front row, to foster independence of rhythms and entrances.
    b. Daily warm-ups should include a scale or other activity performed without conductor, encouraging students to listen and to play together.
    c. Within rehearsals, have selected sections occasionally play passages without conductor, listening to themselves and another section for ensemble.

Recipe:
1. Check for readiness.
   Students should be able to play the piece(s) from beginning to end with correct rhythms and pitches (perhaps two weeks or more before the concert).

2. Play without conductor.
   Play through the piece, with no conductor once they have begun. Encourage students to listen to others and watch each other. In difficult passages, encourage listening to a specific section or sections, as the rhythmic leaders, based on their rhythm. Look for something strong, on the beat, or with clear downbeats.

3. Play in one big circle.
   "Everybody's in the front row!" If your numbers and space allow, this rehearsal forces independent counting, and also makes more players and sections available visually to others. As director, stay on the outside of the circle, and don't conduct! (Clap briefly for the beat if necessary.)

4. Play in small (quartet–quintet) circles.
    Scatter small ensemble circles around the room, with one student or one stand of students from each section in each circle, and simultaneously play the piece. As director, wander around the room, and don't conduct! (Clap briefly for the beat if necessary.)

5. Perform with confidence!
    Students will be more confident in performance, knowing that they can play without conductor, or without the help of section members in front of them or even nearby. This process also reinforces in them the need to know their own part well in order to be a successful ensemble listener and watcher. ➦

Healthy, Fresh String Players

Judy Palac

"Sit up on the front of your chairs! Keep your backs straight! Don't crook your left arm at the wrist. What do you mean, your shoulder hurts? Hold that violin up!"

INGREDIENTS:
Willing, garden-variety young string players in typical sizes and body types
Teacher with a little body awareness

SERVES:
String students and teachers who want to play comfortably and energetically.

TIME NEEDED:
Ten minutes out of every rehearsal or hour practiced.

1. **Preheat muscles to about 102 degrees.**
   Take students through a 3–5 minute warm-up routine. Such activities as miming their favorite sports (shooting baskets, throwing balls, running in place), the hokey-pokey, or other fitness routines work well. Your phys ed teachers or coaches know some, or you can consult Winberg and Salus's *Stretching for Strings*, published by ASTA.

2. **Fit equipment to students.**
   Make sure endpins are long enough, chinrests are high enough, shoulder pads are in place, and that instruments are the right size (too small is better than too large). Chairs should be high enough that feet are firmly on the floor and hips are higher than knees. Seats that are flat or slightly tilted to the front are preferable.

3. **Introduce good dynamic balance (posture) from which to play—stir in regularly!**
   When sitting, students should be sitting squarely on their "sitz bones" (the bony protuberances of the pelvis), with spinal curves preserved—lower back slightly in, upper back slightly out. The shoulders should be over the hips, and the head and spine joint, slightly behind the ears in the middle of the head, should be over all. The back of the chair may be used when students get tired.

4. **Take breaks.**
   Players need to take a break when they've been playing continuously for even 5 minutes. This is especially important during intense rehearsals. The break may consist of simply shaking arms and hands out, or taking a couple of deep breaths, or rolling

shoulders back for a few seconds. Students should be taught to do this on their own when they have long rests, rather than keeping instruments up in "ready" position.

5. **Stretch.**

Players need to stretch when they feel tight, and also when they are finished playing to prevent tightening and cramping. This can be done for a few minutes as part of the rehearsal routine or on their own. The Winberg and Salus book has very good stretching routines.

6. **Distribute the workload.**

A greater number of shorter rehearsals is more productive than concentrated longer ones, and easier on the body. The same is true for individual practice sessions. A sudden increase in practice time and intensity is actually the recipe for injury—the opposite of what we want!

Following this recipe will result in string players who not only have more energy available for their musicianship, but enjoy playing in comfort. Moreover, they'll have the recipe to keep themselves playing healthy for the rest of their lives! Enjoy! ➙●

A Balanced Diet: A Recipe for Balancing Your String Curriculum with Alternative Musical Styles

Bob Phillips

INGREDIENTS:
Students who are ready to have fun and be adventurous
A teacher willing to try new things and step out of his/her comfort zone
Materials—books, recordings, and videos/DVDs

SERVES:
All string students.

- Start by choosing the type or types of music that excite you personally, that you enjoy. Your choice should fit your preferences and your community, whether this be fiddling, jazz, Latin, rock, mariachi, etc. Incorporate this music in your curriculum or start a separate performing ensemble.
- Attend alternative style workshops such as the National ASTA Conference to learn more! There are also summer camps for adults such as the Mark O'Connor Fiddle Camp, Ashokan Fiddle and Dance Camp, the Dusquesne Workshop, and the Vanderbilt Camp. There are many more opportunities. Fiddler magazine maintains a list!
- Attend festivals in your area and introduce yourself to artists. Let them know you are introducing kids to their music and ask if they would serve as a resource. Invite local artists to give workshops or perform either in an assembly or an evening concert.
- Start with your younger students and let the curriculum build from the ground up.
- Take a few interested students to an alternative styles concert with you to generate interest. This may be a professional concert or an outstanding student group in the area.
- Visit guitar shops. They are a great resource of teachers, concerts, instruments, and workshops in other musical styles. Read their bulletin boards.
- Introduce tunes by rote, using the printed music as a memory aid at home. Most folk musics are aural traditions. One benefit of incorporating alternative styles is the development of the ear.
- Build a common repertoire of memorized tunes that students can feel comfortable playing at any time. Continue playing them throughout the year so they stay under the fingers.

- Develop a series of tunes that can be used for pedagogical purposes. For example, "Old Joe Clark" (*Fiddlers Philharmonic*, Alfred Publishing) is perfect to teach low second finger.
- Involve your community by offering to play for local service clubs, nursing homes, school events, and festivals. Let them see that the kids are having a great time playing music, and the community will flock to your side. Have a parent take pictures and write short articles for local papers. Put someone in charge of publicity. Soon everyone will be asking you for your recipe!
- Employ teaching resources such as Alfred's *Philharmonic and String Alternatives* series, Mel Bay's publications, and Homespun Videos. Many music retailers are beginning to present focused areas for resources.

Build a healthy musical experience with a varied and balanced diet of musical styles! Alternative styles of string music bring variety, technical challenge, inspiration, and just plain fun to the string curriculum. They build skills and aid in retaining students. They can also be a means to reach students who might otherwise never try strings or not continue in orchestra. Enjoy these new tastes in your aural diet! ➛

Whipping up a Batch of Tasty Practice Sessions

Rachel Barton Pine

INGREDIENTS:
1 string player (any size), 1 string player's brain, 1 notebook, 1 pen or pencil

SERVES:
The string player, the string player's teacher, and audiences everywhere.

1. **Choose a time commitment for daily practice.**
   Begin by thinking very carefully and realistically about all of your activities and commitments. Determine your priorities, and think creatively how you might organize your schedule to free up a little extra time. Based on this evaluation, decide how many hours you will commit to practicing every day.

2. **List your assignments for the whole week.**
   List in your notebook everything you need to practice in the coming week. The list should include your new solo repertoire, your review pieces, your orchestra pieces, your chamber music, and your technical work (scales, etudes, and exercises).

3. **Create a practice plan for the week.**
   Decide how often you need to practice each piece or exercise. Some items on your list will need work every day, while others can be rotated to alternate days or practiced twice a week. Then assign each piece to specific days of the week. When you have finished, check to be sure that your repertoire is distributed evenly throughout the week.

4. **Create a plan for each day.**
   Next, decide how much time you need to spend on each piece each day, considering its level of difficulty and your priorities. Your brain and muscles will need to be refreshed every so often, so don't forget to schedule breaks. At the end of your practice session, you may reward yourself with a little "free-choice time" by playing a favorite review piece, jamming on a fiddle tune, or experimenting with a rock improvisation.

For example, for a daily practice session of two hours, your notebook might look like this:

Monday

10 min.	scales in key #1
45 min.	new concerto
5 min. break	
15 min.	etudes
15 min.	orchestra piece #1
25 min.	chamber music movement #1
5 min.	free choice

Tuesday

10 min.	scales in key #2
45 min.	new concerto
5 min.	*break*
15 min.	etudes
10 min.	orchestra piece #2
20 min.	chamber music movement #2
10 min.	review piece
5 min.	free choice
Etc.	

Remember that if you begin your practice session with your first piece and don't assign any time limits, you may run out of time before you ever get to your last piece. Keep an eye on the clock!

5. **Create a plan for each piece: time.**
   Depending on the length and difficulty of a particular piece, you might divide it into sections and plan how much time to spend on each section each day. For example:

Monday— 45 min.—new concerto

25 min.	page 1
15 min.	page 2
5 min.	super-hard spot

Tuesday— 45 min.—new concerto

20 min.	page 2
10 min.	page 3
10 min.	page 1
5 min.	super-hard spot

Wednesday— 45 min.—new concerto

20 min.	page 3
10 min.	page 1
10 min.	page 2
5 min.	super-hard spot

Etc.

6. **Create a plan for each piece: goals.**

   Trying to concentrate on too many goals at once will fragment your attention and prevent you from mastering any one of them. Here's how to make your practicing more efficient and effective: Practice slowly. (Very slowly!) Become a "mistake detective" by listening to every note with suspicion. Focus on each side of the body separately before putting both together. (For instance, if you are thinking about intonation, ignore your bow distribution, but when you are concentrating on bow distribution, don't worry about your vibrato.) These habits will maximize your results.

You might record your plans in your notebook like this:

Monday— 45 min.—new concerto

25 min.	page 1
	LEFT SIDE OF THE BODY
	1st step: perfect intonation (one measure at a time, no vibrato)
	2nd step: clean shifts (isolate each)
	3rd step: beautiful vibrato (width, speed, don't leave any notes bare)
	RIGHT SIDE OF THE BODY
	4th step: straight bow, bow fingers, wrist, arm (clear tone, bow changes, string crosses)
	5th step: bow distribution and weight (dynamics and phrasing)
	PUTTING IT ALL TOGETHER
	6th step: rhythm and articulation
	7th step: up to tempo with emotion, one line at a time
	8th step: perform the entire page without stopping

7. **Confirm your plan with your teacher.**

   After you've finished writing down all of the details for this week's practice sessions, ask your teacher to take a look at your notebook and make suggestions.

8. **Adjust and evaluate.**

   Every layer of your practicing plan is a hypothesis. It might turn out that orchestra piece #1 took only 10 minutes, not 15. Your notebook plan is a just a guide, so you can revise it as you go along. Be sure to write down what you actually did, then use this information to create next week's plan and make it even better. You'll soon find that your practice sessions are better organized and more productive.

9. **Keep your commitment.**
   Your muscles need consistent workouts in order to gain strength and improve coordination, and your brain needs consistent reinforcement to secure knowledge in your long-term memory. Skipping a few days and then cramming a week's practicing into the hours before your lesson is no substitute for daily practice, even when the total hours spent are the same. By practicing every single day, you will progress more quickly and retain what you learn.

Intelligent practicing is a habit that will serve you well for the rest of your life! ➤●

Perfection—A Goal Worth Aiming For

Jack Ranney

Early in my teaching career in Ottumwa, Iowa, after a morning assembly given by the band and orchestra, I was greeted in the hall by a fellow teacher who expressed her reaction to the performance. She was extremely complimentary about both ensembles but indicated that she thought the orchestra was much better than the band. Quite surprised with her comment, I asked her what caused her to feel that way. She said, "I'm tone deaf and can't tell one pitch from another—but the orchestra looked great." I thanked her for her comments and each of us went on our way. I will tell you that the band was an outstanding ensemble in every way and that, in my opinion, even though the orchestra was good, it was not better than the band.

INGREDIENTS:
Any number of performers (1 to a full orchestra)
1 audience (the larger the better, consisting of three categories)

SERVES:
Performers striving for a perfect performance, and audience members listening from different perspectives.

Category 1: Audience members that listen only with their eyes:

When I conduct orchestra festivals, I often ask the orchestra members, "What audience do you play for?" While they are thinking, I relay the above story to the orchestra members and explain that there are three types of audiences. The first type is like my colleague in the story. There are the members of your audience that listen only with their eyes. Without realizing it, they will judge your performance on your appearance, posture, bowing, and, what is most important, the level of your energy. They are willing to offer up congratulations based on what they see with their eyes.

Category 2: Audience members that listen with their eyes and ears:

A second group is the audience that listens with its ears, as well as its eyes. These audience members become a little more critical in their observation of the musical performance. Some will be able to judge the intonation of the group while others will even go so far as to evaluate the balance, tone quality, musical accuracy, and various other aspects of the performance. Those making up this audience group might be other music teachers, students from other schools, and, yes, even administrators.

Category 3: Audience members that listen with their eyes, their ears, and their hearts: For several years, I only used the first two audience types in my analogy. However, recently I have added a third ingredient. This is the audience that listens with its heart. This group attends your concert, listens to the performance with great interest, and offers up wonderful praise after it is over. Here you will find your friends, your mothers and fathers, and your grandparents.

So the question is, what audience group do you aim for? Obviously, we want to perform for our family and friends because it gives us an opportunity to share the wonderful world of music. As we work our way through the rehearsal process, I urge students to prepare the music for the audience members that listens with their eyes and ears, as well as their hearts. I also explain to the students that I feel we have one level of performance to aim for. That level is perfection. As humans, we rarely reach the perfect level but we should never stop aiming for it. As students and teachers we should always aim for a level that is beyond that which we have attained. In doing that, we are able to adequately satisfy the expectations of all three audiences.

A Recipe for Conducting a String Orchestra

Donald Schleicher

INGREDIENTS:
An orchestra conductor, experienced or inexperienced and an orchestra, experienced or inexperienced

SERVES:
An orchestra conductor, experienced or inexperienced.

1. **With a large spoon, toss in the music.**
   Begin by revisiting why music was chosen as a career. Demonstrate this passion repeatedly and, in particular, while standing in front of an orchestra. This initial step is especially critical as we get bogged down with workaday struggles such as: repetitive rehearsal moments, pesky parental advice, or annoying bosses.

2. **Follow the composer's recipe.**
   The composer is our guide and our leader. Humility to composer intent is a responsibility as well as a key success factor. We should be prepared for each rehearsal as if it were the concert. Note: It is possible to sneak extra score preparation during hall duty, lunchroom duty, and the like. "Hey, you got five minutes, learn a measure!"

3. **Add an ample amount of calm leadership.**
   The posture of a conductor is a strong communicator. Orchestra musicians, especially the inexperienced ones, fluster easily when led by a noticeably tense conductor. During musically challenging passages such as starts, fermatas, rhythmic or technical complexities, etc., a conductor can easily and without notice fall into poor posture traps such as excessive leaning, physical tension, or uncontrolled gestures. Post-its with the word "relax" strategically placed on your music stand, or in your score, can serve as a simple reminder for a calm posture.

4. **Stir up the art as the craft.**
   It is easy for the conductor to get preoccupied with helping the technical progress of an orchestra. As a result, the craft of our gestures can unknowingly determine how the music sounds. For example, when trying to be effusively clear for a downbeat that is no more than a passing beat in a musical line, the large downbeat shows clarity, yet disturbs linear progression. Striving for gestures driven by musical intent, rather than precision, is the optimum way to enable great music making. Conductor Maurice Abravanel once said, "Never let precision get in the way of the music!"

5. **Drain out confusion.**

Our brightest orchestra musicians notice far more conductor gestures than we think. If a conductor verbally asks for something, but does not physically exhibit the verbal request, confusion can take place. "But, Mr. Smith, do you want us to play what you are showing us or what you are telling us?"

6. **Add a generous amount of gestural variety.**

While attending a Leonard Bernstein conducted concert, this writer overheard an adept definition of conducting from a concertgoer: "Hey, you can kinda tell what the music is going to sound like in advance just by watching him!" Our gestural vocabulary is unlimited in its potential. The music itself is the guide.

7. **Wrap with freedom.**

Maestro Simon Rattle once said to a student conductor: "If you leave them alone, they'll be ok!" This step is a complicated and rewarding mission towards preparing the orchestra to be more musically responsible. A good rehearsal practice is for the conductor to step away from the podium, thus empowering the musicians to listen and fend for themselves. This freedom opens the door for the conductor to return to the podium and serve in a more important artistic capacity.

8. **Cook up good listening.**

The ears of the musicians should always be encouraged to function at a heightened level. In an orchestra, extreme and controlling beats from the conductor can discourage the musicians' ears from hearing at their most alert state. In contrary, more subtle and less controlling gestures, coupled with a *trust the orchestra* approach, can enable an ensemble to acutely listen. The end result will be rewardingly: *big chamber music.*

9. **Season with internal leadership.**

An orchestra is filled with potential leaders. Among the many jobs of the conductor is to find, nurture, and then seek the assistance of these helpers. Further, it is important that these internal leaders be strategically placed throughout the orchestra. Since the back stands of the string section are difficult places to sit, the strategy of placing strong leaders at or near the back can strengthen the whole. Similarly, pairing strong rhythmic leaders on an outside stand with strong tonal leaders on the inside can reinforce a section from within.

Note: this also reduces the need for competitive front-to-back chair placement.

10. **Bake the positive.**

Our rehearsals and concerts should, of course, aspire to be positive experiences. Our nonverbal gestures, however, can unintentionally contain negativity. For example, an intense fortissimo that contains an angry facial expression can be misinterpreted by the musicians. Or, the infamous left hand "piano" gesture—given with good intentions of achieving appropriate balance—can appear to the musicians as a negative command. If the music itself is utilized as the highest priority, gestures can be turned from a negative into a positive.

Lastly, the ingredient of a sense of humor will provide the finishing touch for the climactic icing on the cake! ➼

"That's Correct! Now Repeat, Repeat, Repeat:" A Recipe for Fluency and Permanence

Laurie Scott

INGREDIENTS:
String students, deep breaths, respect and/or acceptance of repetition and drill, recognition of effort, and a pursuit of permanent correctness.

SERVES:
Anyone interested in habituation of correctness and the security and relaxation that can result from repetition.

Often in the development of skills from beginning level to the demonstration of accomplishment, we forget the very ingredient that allows the muscles, ear, and ego to benefit. That ingredient is repetition. Sometimes we feel pressure to either go to the next piece or get ready for the next concert and lose sight of the true measure of accomplishment—performance fluency and permanence of skill. Repetitions of muscle movements need to be correct because practice makes permanent, not perfect. A feeling of "ease" should be accomplished through practice, resulting in confidence and happy music making. In spite of all the positives, it can sometimes be difficult to "sell" the concept of multiple repetitions to students.

By the time many children are in the 1st grade they can count to 100 with few mistakes. It is an accomplishment that is recognized and celebrated. Counting to 100 is a benchmark of early academic accomplishment and the number itself seems mammoth.

Developing Skill Permanence
1. The first step in training respect and/or acceptance of repetition is dispelling the myth that 100 repetitions of anything will "take forever." Students are amazed that you can play a two-octave scale 100 times or land the fourth finger with strong joints 100 times in under 3 minutes. Take time to demonstrate the way great artists practice and emphasize the value of repeating correct muscle movements.

2. Take time during class to hear individuals demonstrate exercises and correct skill performances multiple times. Document changes in speed and fluency and emphasize *how* people play, not *what* they are playing.

3. Use improvement of skill as a measure of success and achievement. Award grades for skill accomplishment and consistency, not just repertoire acquisition. In the beginning stages of study, students should be recognized for demonstrating perfect posture repeatedly as this forms the foundation for all further technical development.

4. Draw attention to fine details of performance related to musicianship and posture. Encourage students to look at their technique under the microscope, noting "how fast," "how high," "what angle," and answering questions related to why things did or didn't work on certain performance trials.

Repeated Repertoire

1. Develop routines and arrange performances that allow repetition of learned repertoire. Choose concert repertoire that includes pieces previously programmed. Familiarity with the repertoire fosters comfort and security in performance and the ability to pay attention to ensemble and musical details.

2. Maintain a "gig book" of pieces that can be used for schoolwide assembly programs, concert preludes, and various community functions. Add to the collection but emphasize growth in musical maturity and tone production as students play the same pieces throughout their years at either the middle or high school.

3. Play previously performed music at every rehearsal so students have the opportunity to work on skill development and permanence without worrying about new notes or fingerings.

4. Develop solo repertoire that *everyone* learns. Motivate students by providing excellent peer and professional models. Repeat the repertoire for each grade level and instrument each year. Students will be motivated through expectation—knowing that they will play certain pieces at each grade level. While students can of course exceed this learning pace and learn more literature, at least all students will have some memorized repertoire that they can play with others or for functions in and out of school. ➤●

Early String Advocacy in the Classroom: Introducing Renaissance and Baroque String Repertoire on Period Instruments to Students

Phillip W. Serna

"What is that strange instrument? Is that a mutant cello? Is that thing a guitar? What is a theorbo? A lute? A viola da what? It has frets? Your bow is funny! Why do you hold your bow like that? Why does the music sound weird? You play on strings made of what? Gut? Yuck!"

INGREDIENTS:

Inquisitive string teachers and students (also music history, theory, and European history teachers and students), enthusiastic performers, and pedagogues equipped with period instruments, photos, recordings, facsimile editions, and a multitude of musical examples and musicological information on style and performance.

OPTIONAL INGREDIENTS (ADD AT YOUR DISCRETION):

Bowed instruments (viola da braccio/violin family and other viola da gamba family instruments), plucked instruments (lute, theorbo, early guitars, etc.), articulation, gut strings, bows and bow materials, bow holds, bowings, chords, consort music, continuo and figured bass, harmony, consonance, dissonance, rhythm, time signatures, tuning, vibrato, ornamentation, phrasing, dance forms, divisions and other variation techniques, national styles, treatises, facsimile editions, etc.

SERVES:

Students in a multitude of educational venues (general music classes, music history classes, music theory classes, history classes, social studies classes), but primarily students in orchestra programs at the high school and middle school level.

1. **Always start with the music.**
   A lot of Renaissance and baroque music for viols and period violin family instruments will sound very alien to the uninitiated listener who has never been exposed to the repertoire before. It is important to let them hear music from diverse genres: from polyphonically dense fantasia repertoire to the most homophonic dance repertoire. Contrasts are essential! Let your students sample as many flavors as possible. Fun is the key to create an enthusiastic atmosphere. Entertain lots of questions from students . . . always!

2. **Explain how early string instruments vary from their modern counterparts (i.e., gut strings, bows and bow materials, instrument construction, etc.).**

Medieval, Renaissance, and baroque music, performed on period instruments, differs significantly from performances on modern instruments. Students must experience the way these differences affect performance. When possible, start with instruments and repertoire that the students will be least familiar with (viols, lute, theorbo, etc.) so that you engage their enthusiasm and curiosity. Being a viola da gamba performer and pedagogue, I always enjoy the curiosity a fretted bowed instrument causes! When applicable, show students the difference of modern versus period instrument construction and materials (i.e., gut strings, bows and bow materials, instrument construction, etc.).

Always insist on students hearing the differences and, when possible, feeling them through hands-on activities. The more a student experiences the sensation of feeling and hearing, the more you can reinforce the differences between the two. If you do not have instruments, use pictures, recordings, make it a sensory experience in any way you can. Also, throw in information on historical context. While you don't want to kill their appetite, you do want to whet it. There is a wealth of musical flavors to be enjoyed here; pick your spices carefully!

3. **Optional: Explain how early fretted bowed string instruments differ from nonfretted ones.**

Touch on the issue of temperament and how it affects intonation, chord structures, etc. Discuss the concept of continuo and how it was used in Renaissance, baroque, and early classical period music. While strings and frets were made of gut, it will allow students to see the flexibility involved with instruments that can make adjustments for pitch. Also, mention the issues of temperament without going into too much detail with the math. Foster an appetite for information—never kill it.

4. **Always keep activities hands-on when possible.**

Nothing enhances the learning process more than hands-on activity. Even if having a number of viols on hand will probably not be feasible (or even one for some students to try), start with giving students a chance at trying a baroque bow hold higher up the bow or have your cellists play without their endpins. Try some of the repertoire. Harmonically dense fantasias may be hard at first, but there are numerous works from the five- and six-part repertoires that would fit a string orchestra setting.

5. **Introduce students to debates on performance, but make sure they do not get too "full" or suffer from information "indigestion!"**

Just because a composer did not write dynamics or articulations, does not mean that they are absent from a performance of Renaissance and baroque repertoire. Bring recordings of modern and period performers for listeners to compare and contrast. Ask the students many questions—you will often be surprised by what they come up with! Remind students that there is a lot of written evidence that elements of performances were completely improvised. Numerous works survive on how to improvise divisions on melodies you are playing, in addition to other forms of ornamentation. Get the authoritative information. Pull out information from surviving written sources. Again, don't do too much here. Avoid indigestion where possible.

6. **Discuss the music and relate it to music they are familiar with.**

   Discuss consort music written for different families of instruments. Consort music for viols, recorders, and sackbuts are not far removed from the string quartet, wind quintet, and brass ensemble literatures. When possible provide music for the students to try. There is a large literature for unspecified instruments, not to mention viol and violin consort repertoire.

7. **Point them to the sources for more information. Lots of tasty morsels to be found here!**

   A lot of students are familiar with private instructions as a source of information. Since many instruments such as the viol and the lute do not have a continuous performance tradition from the medieval, Renaissance, and baroque periods to the present, we have to locate information on how this repertoire would have been performed. This issue is always contentious, since we are dealing with an age before recordings or video documentary material existed. We have only a few sources of information to go on: artistic iconography for medieval sources, but much information in writing. Some of the best source materials we have are original treatises and method books left behind by performers, pedagogues, and composers.

   Never forget facsimile editions of this music as some of it was originally published. A lot of research goes into producing modern editions, and that research is also a great resource to be tapped. Don't overindulge in this area though. Give students a taste and since a large number of students are Internet savvy, point students to resources such as from Early Music America, American Musical Instrument Society, the Viola da Gamba Society of America, and the Lute Society of America. Also there are numerous journals and other Internet sources that might interest them, with additional Internet resources such as Indiana University's Harmonia Radio Show and the numerous podcasts available to satisfy even the smallest cravings. Since time with students is always limited, be clear and concise, and always leave them interested in more.

8. **Sit back and enjoy!**

   While it may not turn every student onto period instrument performers, raising performance practice issues with students will only better inform their performance on modern string instruments. Helping students understand how their instruments and the repertoire evolved, and exposing them to music they have likely never been exposed to, will only enrich their love of string music, no matter where their interests may lead them. Advocacy and outreach is the key. Any performer or advocate of early music will have a lot to offer and gain from interaction with students. As a string teacher, this introduces a large body of works to be discovered to educate and entertain your students. If you have colleagues who play early instruments, get them into your classroom to bring their love of early music to your students. Encourage students to ask many of questions. You'll all have a tasty time getting to know the music as well as the history and theory behind it! ➥

Recipe for Metronome Practice

Peter Slowik

INGREDIENTS:
Metronome (the louder the better!)
A passage you want to perfect
Time (10–15 minutes a day for one to two weeks)

SERVES:
All players from intermediate level on through professional.

BACKGROUND:
Everyone knows that using a metronome can be helpful in establishing the physical and mental discipline it takes to play a complex passage clearly at performance speed. From my experience as a marathon runner it is clear to me that "cross-training," or workouts at different speeds, will lead to greater results than single-speed training.

Working with a metronome is essential because it provides us an outside arbiter for evaluating our progress. Quarter-note-equals-80 (hereafter all metronome markings will go by the number only, e.g., "80") might feel slow one day and fast the next. Only a metronome (analogous to a trainer's stopwatch) can guide us through the physical levels necessary to drill perfection.

As in any kind of cooking, I recommend the very finest ingredients—in this case the very best metronome you can buy. Four suggestions:

1. Loud is really great.
2. Digital is probably better than analog (more speeds!).
3. Volume controls on the beat, subdivision, and total volume can make metronome work more musical.
4. Some degree of programmability is desirable.

In short, the Dr. Beat metronomes by Boss are among the metronomes which model as excellent tools for a musician's development.

The method:
1. Isolate the section that will benefit from metronome work. The section should:
   a. not be more than 30 seconds in length
   b. not encompass a variety of technical or musical problems

2. "Brain-learn" the section. That is, determine solutions to all the physical problems so that the only work needed is good repetition. This should take no more than two to three days.

3. Find your "maximum speed" at which you can perform the passage.
4. Start daily practice at 50 percent of that speed. Play once as perfectly as possible. The slow speed will help you clarify intonation, articulation, musical shape, etc.
5. Increase the metronome approximately 10 percent (on analog metronomes, skip a click).
6. Repeat the increases until you reach the maximum speed for the day—the speed at which things start to fall apart.
7. *Go 10 percent beyond that speed!* This is a crucial step, essential to pushing your limits. Don't overdo this step, though—once is enough!
8. Go back to the 50 percent speed, and repeat the process, with larger increments (maybe 20 percent) this time.
9. As your time and patience allow, or the passage dictates, do it one more time with 30 percent increments.
10. As your final "finish" step for the day, play at only two tempos:
    a. First at 60–65 percent tempo. This should be really solid after all your work, and feel very secure.
    b. Then play at about 90 percent of the final tempo—fast but totally under control. From this repetition you should feel that you have realized the goal of metronome work: to make the fast speed feel as controlled as the slow speed.
11. In successive days, start at a different speeds, for example starting at 60, 61, 62, etc. or at adjacent clicks (60, 63, 60, 63, 66, etc.) on analog metronomes. Adjust your starting speed to always be about 50 percent of the daily maximum speed.
12. Repeat this process until you "own" the passage, and enjoy "serving" it to your dazzled audiences!

Since *your* level determines the speed at which you start and finish, this method works for players of all levels. One more word of advice—you will probably work most effectively with the metronome between 60 and 130 beats per minute or so—feel free to add or subtract subdivisions to make the beat work in this range. ➖●

Setting the Left Hand for Beginning Violin/ Viola Students

David W. Sogin

"Three motions are necessary to the fingers of the left hand: 1) going on and off the string, 2) moving forward and backward on the string, and 3) slipping directly across from one string to another." ~ E. Greene

INGREDIENTS:
Beginning string students who have learned how to stand and support their instrument in both playing and rest positions, enthusiastic string teachers.

SERVES:
Violin and viola students' progress towards successful string playing, their instructors, and good intonation for those who hear their students perform.

1. Make sure the student is ready, can stand in a well-balanced position, and has started working on a great bow hold. Also making sure the instrument is properly sized for the individual student.
2. The student should be set up appropriately to hold the instrument without securing it with their left hand.
3. Next, I play "Hot Potato" with the student. The game is for the student to pretend to reach for the neck of their instrument and then pull away quickly so they don't grab and choke their instrument.
4. I play "Hot Potato" a lot and I begin by using no more then three tapes for young beginners (12 and 3) in a D major pattern and I use only two tapes for adult beginners (1 and 2) again using a D major pattern.
5. For thumb placement, begin by setting the fingers where they need to go and then let the thumb accommodate them. The thumb needs to be as if it is on the side of the instrument and not holding the instrument. In general the thumb needs to be opposite the first or second fingers. Playing "Hot Potato" allows for this natural accommodation.
6. Instead of placing all fingers down in a block, I introduce the fingers one at a time. I play the lift game with beginners, asking them to think of lifting the fingers rather than putting them down. That is, with first finger, touch and pick up, touch and pick up . . .
7. I continue this with the second and third fingers in that order, building a D major scale.
8. The first, second, and third fingers contact the string on the part of the finger closest to the thumb. I sometimes place a small pencil mark on the nail of a student's finger

to show where to line the fingers up on the string. Setting the hand this way seems to predict better vibrato, intonation, and overall shape of the hand.

9. Assess your students by looking at their check points: 1) wrist should be relaxed but make sure it is in a straight line and not collapsed, 2) make sure the thumb is accommodating the fingers, and 3) the fingernails point toward the bridge. Finally, have your students identify models of both good and bad hand positions and offer a reward for the most flexible "iron hand" in the class.

Summary:
Setting the left hand at the very beginning will give the student access to good intonation, a successful attempt at developing a professional vibrato, and ultimately the opportunity to make beautiful music by themselves and with others. ━●

Out-of-Tune Low Second Finger Cake

David Tasgal

INGREDIENTS:
One all-natural second finger typically found about midway between his neighbors on the violin fingerboard (if you can find such a finger!)

SERVES:
All vulnerable life forms within earshot.

First Layer (in which second finger becomes a dog):
Place first finger on string in usual location.
Place second finger touching first finger.
Place third finger touching second finger (all three fingers snuggled together).
First finger is the *house*, second finger is the *family dog*, third finger is the *kid*.
It's time for the kid to go to school. Third finger slides up string to his usual place or even farther. Uh-oh! Second finger starts to follow third finger.
Teacher must say playfully "Oh DOG, where do you think YOU'RE going?"
Or, "Nice try, dog. You can't go to school."

Second Layer (in which second finger becomes a train):
Place first and third fingers as usual (or even farther apart). They are train stations.
Second finger slides on string back and forth all the way between his neighbors, who must not move. Why? Because they're STATIONary!

Icing (in which second finger becomes a baseball player):
A low second finger that is too high or a high second finger that is too low should be asked the following *baseball trivia question:* "What happens to base runners who get caught in between bases?" ➡

Selling Strings: How to Build School and Community Support for Orchestra Programs

Laura Mulligan Thomas

"We are short on classroom space this year, so you'll be teaching strings in the custodian's closet." "Yeah, my kid wanted to play violin but I told him I couldn't stand to hear all that squeaking." "You're our new orchestra director? I didn't know we had an orchestra!"*

Ouch! What is wrong with this picture?

String teachers know that violins don't have to produce squeaky sounds, and that playing great orchestral literature is exciting, noble, and far from nerdy! How should one respond to misperceptions about string playing that may lead to lack of support for a school orchestra? How does a string teacher get from the custodian's closet to Carnegie Hall? Here's the recipe:

INGREDIENTS:
Outstretched hand
Wide variety of repertoire
Logo
Horn to toot
"Bragging rights" list, complete with photos
Big smile, and lots of faith

SERVES:
Thousands, several hundred at a time; lasts forever.

1. Reach out. Get to know your school staff, introduce yourself to the superintendent, the school board, the mayor, council members, your neighbors, and especially, your students' parents! Create a booster club and give parents responsibilities, support, and appreciation. You'll be amazed at what an organized group of motivated parents can accomplish. Be a vital part of your school's "team," and your teammates will support you in kind.

2. Create a catchy logo for your orchestra, and use it everywhere! Combine an interesting font with musical clip art, or pay a graphic designer to do it for you. Enlarge the logo and frame it on the wall of your classroom. Put it on letterhead, t-shirts, static stickers, keychains, folders, and anything else you can think of! Kids love feeling that they belong to a group, and having a graphic "identity" is an important part of that.

3. Select music that will appeal to a wide audience—movie theme music, Motown classics, and jazz/bluegrass, as well as the three Bs. Stretch your students by giving them serious, challenging, as well as accessible, lighter pieces for each concert. Program something for everyone!

4. Keep a running list of your students' and program's accomplishments. Share it and e-mail photos frequently to administrators and parents so that they are aware of, proud of, and informed about your program. Make sure that information and all of your concert dates get in the school newsletter, as well as the local paper.

5. Seek opportunities for your students to play in public in small groups and as a large ensemble. Concerts are great, but sending a student string quartet to provide prelude music for PTO, school board, and faculty meetings will expose your program to more people who are the decision makers. Perform the national anthem at school or community sporting events, play at "grand openings," send quartets out to play in weddings, receptions, etc.

6. Smile every time you introduce your fine young musicians, and say a word or two of interest about the music, what skills you are focusing on in class, or even what the musicians do outside of the orchestra room. SELL it!

*These are actual quotes spoken to the author in her first year of teaching. Her program is no longer a secret in her community. Check it out at www.chsorchestra.org! ➻

Recipe for Teaching "Twinkle, Twinkle Little Star," Suzuki Style, on the Viola/Violin

Gwendoline Thornblade

INGREDIENTS:

1 recording of Suzuki Book 1 pieces listened to at least once a day
1 correctly drawn foot chart (depicting rest position/playing position)
1 concert bow with instrument in rest position
Correctly formed bow "hold/balance" (with thumb in beginner position)
Correct viola/violin placement posture using head weight for balance
Correct left hand placement, with elbow swung forward and viola/violin resting on thumb side, with no left thumb pinching
Place all essential ingredients in a studio

SERVES:

1 motivated student with a tuned viola/violin with correctly positioned three tapes (close 2/3 pattern).
1 motivated parent with a tuned viola/violin with correctly positioned three tapes (close 2/3 pattern), note book/tape-recorder/video, and Suzuki Book 1.
1 motivated teacher with a tuned viola/violin.

Preparation

- Identify the four fingers of the left hand with left finger/thumb tapping games on the thumb side (inside corners) of the four fingers (e.g., telephone numbers 132-4312).
- Identify the A and E strings.
- Teach silent string crossings with the bow E-A-E-A using ti-ti-ti-ti ta-ta rhythm ("Mississippi Hot Dog").
- Identify F♯ (1 on E) by teaching E-F♯-E (using "Mississippi Hot Dog").
- Review the alphabet A-B-C-D forwards, and backwards D-C-B-A.
- Place D (3 on A) by the "swing/drop" exercise (i.e., swing left elbow forward to carry third finger to the A string, then drop third finger on D).
- Prepare C♯ by touching D with second finger and when ready, lift off D.
- Prepare B by placing first finger on first tape and when ready lift off C♯.
- Prepare A by lifting off first finger.

Assembly

- Learn only four notes at a time.
- Learn "A" section (A-E-F♯-E-D-C♯-B-A).

- Learn "B" section and repeat it (E-D-C♯B).
- Repeat "A" section.
- Play with piano introduction and accompaniment.

Presentation
- Assemble all relatives and friends, seated on chairs.
- Dress artist performers in the smartest but comfortable outfits.
- Print programs.
- Welcome the audience.
- Perform "Twinkle" (can be videoed unobtrusively by a parent/friend).
- Acknowledge overwhelming applause with a concert bow and graciously thank the pianist.
- Pose for photographs with the teacher and pianist.
- Greet the audience while enjoying the post-concert reception.

This recipe has been a great favorite in our household and has been repeated many times! ➘

Keeping Elementary Strings Students Motivated

Stephanie Trachtenberg

Sports, dance, day care, high-tech amusements at home filling the kids "free time." Can we get them interested in strings and keep them interested in staying in the program?

INGREDIENTS:
Enthusiastic children who want to learn to play a string instrument

SERVES:
Students in grades 4, 5, 6, and their teachers.

1. **Recruiting**
   Make your presentation fun and flashy!

2. **Environment**
   Create a classroom that is friendly and creative.

3. **Group Lessons**
   Students who watch others play are more stimulated to perform.

4. **Home Concerts**
   Encourage home concerts for family, friends, even pets—this is always a great motivator.

5. **More Performances**
   As proficiency increases, perform for kindergarteners. Older students can perform "Spooky Songs" in October, "Patriotic Songs" for Veteran's Day in November, "Seasonal Strings!" in December (live performances or videotaped for school television network).

6. **Other Ways to Make Music Fun**
   Take part in school-related activities. Social Studies: "Colonial Day Musicians," "Medieval Musicians," "Pioneer Fiddlers."

   Do a Mardi Gras parade with the primary grades.

   Provide music for the PTA Volunteer Tea, Installation of Student Council officers, Boy Scout /Girl Scout special events.

   Perform in district festivals and perform at a local mall.

7. **Add Some Pizzazz**
   Have a concert theme and use props.

   Make the students in the audience say, "I can't wait to join next year!"

   Keep your program visible throughout the year. Take digital photographs of students performing and have them appear regularly in school newsletters and on the school home page on the Internet. With high visibility, the students will be motivated to want to be a part of your program.

"Bassic" Recipe for Good Bass Playing

Mike Trowbridge

INGREDIENTS:
Bass players who would like to have good playing position and good tone. Teachers who would like to see bass players in their class/orchestra with good playing position and good tone.

SERVES:
Bass players and teachers of bass players, grades 5-12.

"Bassic" Bass Playing Position
1. To measure the correct height for the bass: hold the bass with left hand at the crook of the neck and put your arm straight out . . . the left hand should be level with the shoulder.
2. Put the corner of the bass in the belly (not the side of the bass). This allows the bass to resonate.
3. Be able to balance the bass using only one finger of the left hand (be careful with this one).
4. Slow dance with the bass. Not the way they danced in the 1890s but the way kids dance today . . . very close. The side of the player's head should be close to the neck of the bass and the left hand.
5. Be able to hug the bass (left and right hands can meet at the end of the fingerboard).
6. Be able to touch your nose with your index finger of your left hand while holding the bass (in first position).

Left Hand Position
1. The left hand should look like you are throwing a football.
2. The left hand needs to look like you are holding a can of soda or a bottle of water.
3. Put the thumb behind the neck.
4. Do not let the fingers collapse (you cannot hold a bottle of water with collapsed fingers).

Holding the Bow
The (French) bow grip should be the way your hand is when someone hands you a book (I always use a method book to demonstrate)—with the thumb bent a little bit.

Bowing
1. The bow has to be at a right angle to the string.
2. When the teacher says "more bow" to the class, the bass player needs to use less bow.
3. Use right arm weight to get more sound.
4. Use less bow to get more sound.

5. Too much bow on fast passages can get a wispy sound.
6. Make sure that the string is vibrating to get the best sound out of the bass.
7. The higher the note—the bow should move closer to the bridge.
8. The higher the note—the bow should move faster.

Pizzicato
1. The right hand thumb should be on the side of the fingerboard.
2. Use the side of your index finger to do pizz., not the tip—unless you want a blister or are playing "ppp."

Tuning
1. Use harmonics to tune. Start with the A on the D string in III position (fourth finger).
2. Then the first finger on the A string in III position.
3. Then use the A string to tune the E string (fourth and first fingers again).
4. Then use the D string to tune the G string (first finger on the D string and fourth finger on the G string).

Other
1. When using bass rosin, draw the bow only in a down bow direction.
2. Carlsson Swedish bass rosin and Pop's bass rosin are the main two brands of rosin. Some players like to use Pop's in the winter because it is very soft and Carlsson in the summer because it is a harder rosin.
3. Use a crutch tip instead of a rock stop (it's very inexpensive). You might have to put a washer or a copper pipe cap inside the crutch tip.
4. The use of an "egg pin" makes it easier to balance the bass. ➤

Resources
Lemur Music "World's most complete source for the double bassist" 1-800-246-BASS
   www.lemurmusic.com
Nouvelle Technique de la Contrebasse–Editions Musicales by Francois Rabbath (Alphonse Leduc)
Progressive Repertoire for the Double Bass by George Vance Vol. 1, 2, and 3 (Carl Fischer)
New Method for the Double Bass by F. Simandl (Carl Fischer)
30 Etudes for the String Bass by F. Simandl (Carl Fischer)

A Recipe for Using Patterns to Develop Bowing Style—Bowing Patterns, and their Musical Applications

Kristin Turner

INGREDIENTS:
Sections in a string orchestra attempting to develop their bowing styles
Warm-up patterns that help develop correct physical motions for each stroke
Applications to musical examples

SERVES:
All students wishing to match bow strokes within their sections and to play music with correct style.

1. **Begin bowing skills free from left hand involvement.**
   Have students establish the correct motion for each of the stylistic strokes, i.e., déta-ché, martelé, spiccato, ricochet, or sautillé, with repeated drill on open strings until everyone plays with an accurate and easy motion. Be sure each section matches their strokes exactly for each style drill to obtain the optimum uniformity of stroke.

2. **Repeat drills daily until right hand and arm motions are well established.**
   Incorporate the bowing style drills into the orchestra warm-up period and have students play them daily to form an automatic physical response to the need for one or other of the strokes. Students will benefit by consistent repetition. Their right hands and arms "learn" the various strokes "by heart," allowing the student to use them whenever they are called for in the music without conscious thought to the motion of the bow.

3. **As the patterns become well established in the right hand, gradually add different left hand notes.**
   Once the right hand motion has become stable and predictable, fingering may gradually be added. At first, drills may include multiple repetitions of pitches in a scale or other melodic pattern. As dexterity improves, the repetitions may be gradually reduced until at length the students can perform their bow stroke on scales, arpeggios, or technical passages with one note to a bow. Many times, these drills must be practiced at tempo to produce the correct motion in the stroke. If the speed may be varied, students will eventually, through drills at various tempi, be in control of the bow stroke regardless of the speed required.

4. **Taking students' physical characteristics into account may facilitate learning with respect to individual differences.**

Naturally, a student's physiological characteristics will enter into his/her ability to use the bow in a certain way. For instance, students with short arms and fingers will approach their tasks from a different perspective than those with long arms and fingers. An inventive teacher can help in this regard by teaching each individual to accomplish the physical requirements by adapting their technique to fit their physical uniqueness.

5. **Apply the strokes to musical examples.**

Once the group has developed good habits with regard to several of the major strokes, they can begin to apply them to a specific piece of music. For instance, if a group that has become proficient in the spiccato stroke begins to play a piece by Mozart, they can refine and adapt their skills to fit the melodic and rhythmic patterns they encounter in the music. Further, the group may begin to understand that such a stroke is common practice not only for Mozart, but for other classical composers, such as Haydn and Beethoven as well. By making such transfers, the students develop their musical judgment and sophistication. They will be making excellent music as well as learning to perform the pitches and rhythms of their pieces.

6. **Challenge students to transfer information.**

When students feel comfortable applying the various bow strokes to specific pieces of music, a creative teacher may want to challenge them to exercise their own judgment in deciding what styles would be appropriate in a new situation. Letting the group discuss the music and agree on a style can allow them an opportunity to make knowledge transfers themselves and begin to apply their knowledge of basic bowing styles to the type and period of music they are playing. Developing a group of astute, thinking musicians can be a rewarding process. Enjoy! ➤●

An Effective Recruiting Demonstration

Mary Wagner

The recruiting demonstration should be fun for all involved. Use your creativity to come up with a dynamite program to encourage children in your school to join the orchestra.

You can make the demonstration so attractive that even students previously not interested in the orchestra will change their minds.

INGREDIENTS:
An organized demonstration that has been advertised within the school, set up in advance with classroom teachers and the school administration, and is very upbeat!

SERVES:
Future string students and string teachers seeking new students.

1. Organize an interactive recruiting demonstration.
    It can feature student performers or you can demonstrate all of the instruments by yourself. The students in the audience should have some interaction with you.

2. Make up a game similar to Jeopardy, Name That Tune, or Who Wants to Be a Millionaire. Get a large science poster board and make a game board. Let's use Jeopardy as an example.

    One column can ask questions about the string instrument family, such as "Name the smallest or highest-pitched string instrument."

    Another column or two can be "Audio Questions" where you demonstrate on each instrument. The students have to tell you what type of music it is or name the piece. Here is your chance to play a little on each instrument. Play a line of a classical piece, a couple movie themes, a Broadway tune they would be familiar with, a TV theme, a fiddle tune, a patriotic song, and a jazz or blues tune. The last column can be questions about the program at your school.

3. At the demonstration—divide the class into two teams.
    Get a scorekeeper from each team and play on! The students love the competition and trying to identify the type of music. This gives the teacher the perfect opportunity to explain all the types of music we play.

4. After the game, let students "try" the instruments.
    Get a couple violins and a viola ready to pass through the audience. Show them which string is the A string. Play "Pop Goes the Weasel" on your instrument and have them

provide the "pop" by gently plucking the open A at the right time. Then pass the instrument to the next student. This gives them an instrument in their hand.

5. Conclude the demonstration by handing every student a registration sheet.
6. While the students are leaving the room you can look at their hands and say, "You'd make a great cellist."
7. Or, buy one of the movie books that comes with a CD and play along with it while the students are on their way out of the room.

Recruiting really takes place daily. As you walk through the school, acknowledge your students in passing. Keep your classroom attractively decorated, greet the students with an upbeat smile, and keep your program highly visible. Think of the recruiting demonstration as only the beginning of a long relationship!

Notes

Notes

Notes

Notes

Notes

MORE GREAT BOOKS FROM
MEREDITH MUSIC